BECOMING A
BETTER
SCIENCE TEACHER

BECOMING A
BETTER
SCIENCE TEACHER

8 Steps
to High Quality Instruction
and Student Achievement

ELIZABETH HAMMERMAN
Foreword by Dave Youngs

CORWIN PRESS
A SAGE Publications Company
Thousand Oaks, California

For information:

Corwin Press
A Sage Publications Company
2455 Teller Road
Thousand Oaks, California 91320
www.corwinpress.com

Sage Publications Ltd.
1 Oliver's Yard
55 City Road
London EC1Y 1SP
United Kingdom

Sage Publications India Pvt. Ltd.
B-42, Panchsheel Enclave
Post Box 4109
New Delhi 110 017 India

Printed in the United States of America

Library of Congress Cataloging-in-Publication Data

Hammerman, Elizabeth.
Becoming a better science teacher : 8 steps to high quality instruction and student achievement / Elizabeth Hammerman.
    p. cm.
Includes bibliographical references and index.
ISBN 1-4129-2660-2 (cloth : acid-free paper) — ISBN 1-4129-2661-0 (pbk. : acid-free paper)
    1. Science—Study and teaching—Methodology. 2. Curriculum planning. 3. Mathematics—Study and teaching—Standards. 4. Science teachers—Training of. I. Title.
Q181.H147 2006
507.1—dc22

2006002889

This book is printed on acid-free paper.

06   07   08   09   10   9   8   7   6   5   4   3   2   1

Acquisitions Editor:	Jean Ward
Editorial Assistant:	Jordan Barbakow
Production Editor:	Kristen Gibson
Copy Editor:	Eugenia Orlandi
Typesetter:	C&M Digitals (P) Ltd.
Indexer:	Sheila Bodell
Proofreader:	Andrea Martin
Cover Designer:	Michael Dubowe

Contents

Foreword

*B*ecoming a Better Science Teacher could appropriately be subtitled *Successful Science for All* since in it science educator and author Elizabeth Hammerman provides a powerful vision for successful science education that, while focusing on teachers, ultimately impacts students' learning of science. To make this vision a reality, Hammerman shows teachers many ways to make high quality curriculum and instruction a part of their everyday approach to science teaching. This focus is especially appropriate in light of recent research. For example, Horizon Research's 2003 *Looking Inside the Classroom* study found that only 15 percent of the K–12 science and mathematics classes in a nationally representative sample of 364 classrooms were judged to have high quality instruction, while 59 percent were judged to be low in quality. Hammerman addresses these disturbing statistics in a positive way by highlighting the indicators of high quality curriculum and instruction that provide successful science teaching and learning. After reviewing and synthesizing current research and national standards in science, she presents eight indicators of high quality teaching. She notes that by themselves these indicators are not enough to ensure successful science. Instead, they provide a foundation for helping teachers develop both science content knowledge and science pedagogical content knowledge as they collaborate in a science unit-development process. Hammerman then weaves the eight indicators of high quality together with eight practical steps for building high quality instructional materials that inform high quality instruction.

While designed for K–12 teachers, this book should also be of interest to administrators and curriculum specialists. Science educators working with pre-service teachers will find it an excellent resource for science methods courses.

To summarize, the exciting vision for successful science teaching presented in this book promotes a standards- and research-based approach. This approach incorporates effective pedagogy and best practices; tools for thinking and meaning making; assessment that guides instruction; and supportive and safe learning environments. The book also reinforces the vision for high quality science instruction depicted in national standards; includes strategies to meet the needs of diverse student populations; and supports the planning and implementation of high quality, standards-based instructional units. It is a welcome addition to the field of science education.

Dave Youngs, ScEdD
Director, AIMS Education Foundation
Science Educator, Fresno Pacific University

Preface

High quality teaching of science is within the reach of all teachers. Armed with a good understanding of the messages of the standards, an adequate knowledge base of concepts, and high quality units and lessons to guide practice, K–12 teachers can deliver the quality of instruction that raises student achievement in science. From the primary teachers who teach science only one period per day to the 12th grade science teachers who are looking for new ways to make concepts more accessible to a broader range of students, this book is intended to guide teachers through a process for reaching their educational goals.

PROFESSIONAL DEVELOPMENT FOR LEARNING AND CHANGE

Good teachers have always sought to improve their own content knowledge and repertoire of strategies on the road to becoming master teachers. The current educational focus on high priority standards for all learners and high stakes testing for accountability has placed new demands that make professional growth a requirement for all teachers in order to acquire the tools and strategies they need to develop deep understandings of concepts and strengthen thinking and problem-solving skills in a diverse population of learners.

Educational theories and research in effective teaching and learning point to a range of student learning styles, human capabilities, and gender and cultural learning preferences and offer an array of instructional strategies that promote student achievement. Such insights have far-reaching implications that offer teachers new understandings of the kinds of knowledge and skills, tools, and resources that will enhance learning.

Teachers and administrators know that ongoing professional development can be a key ingredient in the quest for higher student achievement. Courses, workshops, and conferences, although helpful in providing an awareness of problems and suggestions for effective teaching and learning, often do not offer teachers clear bridges for the transfer of new learning to the specific conditions of their classrooms and needs of their students. They do not offer a clear, comprehensive approach for changing teaching that translates to success for teachers and higher student achievement.

Teacher time is precious. Often the missing component in professional growth is the opportunity to apply new knowledge to practice in a timely manner with the support of their learning communities, in combinations that include coaches, content mentors and colleagues, team members, study groups, instructional leaders, and support staff.

Dr. Anne Lieberman, Professor of Education at Columbia University, supports the idea that professional growth in teaching is best supported by collaborative study and coaching around improved practice.

> The conventional view of staff development as a transferable package of knowledge to be distributed to teachers in bite-sized pieces needs radical transformation and rethinking. It carries not only a limited conception of teacher learning, but one grounded in a set of assumptions about teacher, teaching, and the process of change that does not match current research or practice. (Grimmett & Neufield, 1994; Little, 1993; McLaughlin & Talbert, 1993; Wood, 1992, in *Practices That Support Teacher Development: Transforming Conceptions of Professional Learning,* 1995; Innovating and Evaluating Science Education: NSF Forums, 1992–94, p. 67, www.nsf.gov/pubs/1995/nsf95162/nsf_ef.pdf)

USES FOR *BECOMING A BETTER SCIENCE TEACHER*

Becoming a Better Science Teacher is rooted in research-based indicators of high quality teaching and research-based strategies that enable teachers to apply knowledge directly to effective classroom practice. When teachers work collaboratively with other teachers in the process of developing or modifying instructional units to meet the standards of "high quality," they take a critical first step toward change by improving the quality of teaching needed to increase student achievement. The research-based model offered in this book has been used successfully by preservice and in-service teachers and in site-based professional development initiatives to:

- reinforce teacher understanding of standards-based concepts and the goals of science education
- learn new content, methods, and strategies for instruction and assessment
- gain confidence in teaching science as inquiry
- create rich learning environments and make better use of instructional time

In addition, teachers are better able to:

- align standards with instruction and assessment
- use a learning cycle to facilitate the learning process

- ask probing questions, promote discussion, and focus on making meaning and applications of learning to technology and society
- use classroom assessments to gather evidence of student achievement and to inform instruction (AAAS, 1993; Hammerman & Musial, 1995; Jarrett, 1997; NRC, 1996)

OVERVIEW OF CHAPTERS

Part I: Creating a Vision for Successful Science

The first two chapters create a vision for understanding science standards and the goals of science education. These chapters provide a rationale for classroom practice that is based on the work that scientists do and the ways scientists think and act and create an awareness of high quality teaching that is applied throughout the book.

Understanding Standards

The work of science professionals defines the nature of science and describes the role of inquiry-based science in uncovering and discovering the mysteries of the universe. The concepts and principles of the science disciplines inform national and state standards that come under the headings of the Nature of Science, as well as Life Science, Earth/Space Science, and Physical Science. The standards also address the skills and dispositions for K–12 science and identify important goals for the development of the scientifically literate citizen.

High Quality Science Education

Well-designed instructional materials can be used to inform and guide the delivery of high quality instruction in the classroom. A research-based set of indicators of high quality curriculum and instruction are identified for use in the design or modification of standards-based units and lessons to enhance student achievement.

Part II: Giant Steps to High Quality Teaching

Pedagogical Content Knowledge

Throughout Chapters 3–8 a strong case is made for the importance of content knowledge as well as pedagogical content knowledge for effective teaching and learning. Pedagogical content knowledge includes, in the words of Lee Shulman (1986):

the most useful forms of (content) representation . . . the most powerful analogies, illustrations, examples, explanations, and demonstrations— in a word, the ways of representing and formulating the subject that makes it comprehensible for others. (Gess-Newsome & Lederman, 1999, p. 4)

Pedagogical content knowledge is operationally defined in this book through the identification of indicators of high quality science teaching and their application to a process for the development (or modification) of instructional materials to inform and guide instruction.

Creating Blueprints for High Quality Teaching

Indicators of high quality and the steps in the unit development process are aligned in Chapters 3 through 8. These chapters describe a process for creating "blueprints" to guide the delivery of high quality classroom instruction. The indicators of high quality serve as beacons that guide the process.

Table P.1   Eight Steps to High Quality Teaching

Chapter	Indicators of High Quality Teaching	Steps for Developing High Quality Units and Lessons
3	**Steps One–Three** Address clear and appropriate learning goals Build concepts and principles Develop skills and practices dispositions valued by the scientific community	**Steps One–Three** 1. Select a topic or theme from the state or local framework for science education for your grade level. Research and review content information about the topic. 2. Select a set of key concepts and principles appropriate for the grade level around which the unit will be developed. • Design one or more graphic organizers to show relationships between concepts or concept categories for the unit. 3. Consider process skills of science, critical and creative thinking skills, and dispositions to include and emphasize.
4	**Step Four** Accommodates diversity through meaningful contexts	**Step Four** Create a context for meaningful learning. • Consider various types of contexts for the development of high quality instruction. • A sample unit in a cultural context is included.

Table P.1 (Continued)

Chapter	Indicators of High Quality Teaching	Steps for Developing High Quality Units and Lessons
5	**Step Five** Includes varied methods that engage and challenge students intellectually and address prior learning, misconceptions, and new learning Embeds strategies that allow students to develop new or modified thinking frames with links to their own lives, technology, and issues relevant to their community, state, nation, and world	**Step Five** Research learning activities and experiences. Modify existing activities or design new activities. • Use a consistent format for crafting each instructional activity and experience. • Include multiple and varied methods and strategies for meeting the needs of learners. • Consider activities and experiences for relearning and for extended learning.
6	**Step Six** Develops thinking and problem-solving skills by using questioning and other strategies for students to make sense of what they are learning	**Step Six** Include a variety of ways for students to frame thought, link new learning to prior learning, and make connections to their lives, technology, and society. • Develop a student notebook that reflects what students will design, do, record, write, research, and so forth throughout the unit. • Frame thought and show understanding and meaning through visuals, performances, products, and so forth.
7	**Step Seven** Incorporates a well-designed assessment system to monitor and guide the learning process and to provide frequent feedback to students about their learning	**Step Seven** Design a rich assortment of formative assessments. • Establish rubrics to enable students to self-assess. • Use assessment data to assess effectiveness of unit.
8	**Step Eight** Utilizes equipment, materials, and resources for enhancing learning and providing a challenging learning environment	**Step Eight** Consider resources, equipment, and materials that will be needed for effective instruction. Consider management strategies and safety issues.

Applying the Process

Chapter 9 provides a summary of the process for developing high quality instructional units or for modifying existing instructional units and offers examples that were created using the process. The Eight Steps for developing high quality instructional materials are applied to an intermediate grade unit on plants. A unit on rocks and minerals for the intermediate/early high school level is provided to show how the model may be used as a tool for critiquing and modifying instructional materials.

USING AN I.D.E.A. APPROACH TO METACOGNITION

Becoming a Better Science Teacher uses a metacognitive approach where learners are presented with new information and given opportunities to develop or strengthen knowledge and skills related to principles of effective teaching and practices for improving student achievement. Opportunities to follow each stage of the I.D.E.A. Approach are embedded within the chapters.

I   Introduce

D   Discuss

E   Elaborate and Extend

A   Apply and Assess

Introduce

Each chapter begins with an inquiry question related to the topic, which is followed by information in the form of standards, concepts, research findings, models, questionnaires, inventories, best practices, and activities that relate to effective teaching and learning in science.

Discuss

Questions that elicit "thought and discussion" follow content. Through the discussion process, understandings and misconceptions are identified, beliefs and practices are challenged, and action plans for learning or applying new ideas are generated. Discussion is an important part of the process of building a greater understanding of science education and of developing greater confidence in one's ability to teach inquiry-based science.

Elaborate and Extend

Following discussion and reflection, additional information is provided, Web sites or resources are cited, and activities are offered to enable the learner to probe deeper into the main ideas of the chapter. Participation in activities or laboratory experiences, research, or field experiences are just some of the many ways learners can extend or enhance understanding prior to making applications to classroom instruction.

Apply and Assess

In addition to reflecting on current practices and learning new concepts and strategies, learners are challenged to apply new knowledge and best practices to the development of new products, to the modification of existing products, or to their classroom teaching. Continuous assessment of the effectiveness of the classroom applications is critical to the development of new models of effective practice for future use.

ACKNOWLEDGMENTS

The focus of many exciting years of work with professional colleagues, administrators, and teachers has been to instill a love of science and scientific literacy in K–12 students through "better science teaching". This book is dedicated to all who have participated in that journey and contributed in so many ways to the knowledge, insights, and models that are shared here.

I want to thank Jean Ward for her belief in this project and Corwin Press editors and staff, not only for their professional expertise, but for their friendly manner, willing advice, and continuous support.

I am extremely grateful to the reviewers for their time and recommendations. Their obvious professional expertise related to effective teaching and learning, and their generous sharing of ideas enabled me to clarify and refine important messages in the book.

Corwin Press gratefully acknowledges the contributions of the following reviewers.

Diann Musial, EdD
Distinguished Teaching Professor
Northern Illinois University
DeKalb, IL 60115

Gary L. Willhite, PhD
Teacher Educator
Southern Illinois University
Carbondale, IL

Dr. Marian White-Hood
Principal
Prince George's County Public Schools
Upper Marlboro, MD

Bena Kallick, PhD
Educational Consultant
Westport, CT 06880

Introduction

In a standards-based educational climate, classroom teachers want to be assured that the concepts, skills, and dispositions they are teaching address the standards upon which national, state, and local assessments are based. They want to know that they are adequately preparing their students for success on a variety of measures of learning and for success in life.

The model presented in this book has been developed around a research-supported belief that student achievement in science is highly dependent on four major factors:

1. A knowledgeable and capable teacher

2. High quality instructional materials, equipment, and resources

3. Pedagogical content knowledge

4. A safe and rich environment for learning

By offering insight into the characteristics of high quality teaching and meaningful learning, this book provides a vision of what teachers need to know and be able to do to increase student achievement in science.

CHANGING PERSPECTIVES AND NEW APPROACHES

Standards-Based Curriculum

Teachers often hear the message that "the text and instructional materials are not the curriculum; the state course of study or local curriculum guide is the curriculum." The practice of using "standards" to guide instruction is new to teachers who have relied on texts or commercial products to guide them.

To feel comfortable in a standards-based climate, teachers need a good understanding of the national, state, and district standards that define their science curriculum. Further, they need to understand the important concepts and principles inherent in the standards and the ways the instructional materials and strategies they use address standards.

Key Concepts and Principles and Instructional Materials and Strategies

Inquiry-Based Learning

Science standards endorse inquiry as the approach through which the concepts and principles, skills, and dispositions of science should be taught. Yet, teachers are still asking: What is inquiry? How can inquiry be used effectively? How can the instructional materials that I have to teach science be used in an inquiry approach?

The well-defined science curriculum offers not only the framework for what to teach, but also how to teach. Lessons built around an inquiry-based format address important concepts and include valuable strategies to guide meaningful classroom teaching.

High Quality Curriculum and Instruction

It is not necessary to develop a new curriculum to incorporate the messages in this book. There are many well-designed and creative instructional materials available to which to apply the model. One just needs to attend a state or national Science Teachers Association Conference to view the vast array of products and resources available for K–12 teachers. A catalog of government-sponsored science and technology Web sites is available at http://www .scitechresources.gov/

Information in the areas of Arctic and Antarctic; astronomy and space; biology; chemistry; Earth and environment; education; engineering; mathematics; nanoscience; and physics is available at www.nsf.gov/news/classroom.

Commercially available instructional materials and curriculum projects may not align perfectly with the goals and standards of a state or school system. But, a good understanding of standards and concepts, together with an awareness of indicators of high quality, will enable curriculum designers and teachers to assess instructional materials and add or modify units, activities, experience, resources, and assessments, as needed, to align their instructional programs with state and local standards and provide "blueprints" for effective classroom instruction.

About the Author

 **Elizabeth Hammerman** is a dedicated Science Educator. Her background includes teaching science at the middle school and high school levels and teaching preservice and inservice teachers. As a professor, project director, and workshop facilitator, she has taught K–8 science methods courses for seven universities, co-directed grant projects to enhance the quality of K–12 teaching and assessment, served as a Math/Science Consultant for seven counties, and provided professional development for K–8 teachers in hands-on science, effective teaching, standards alignment, and classroom assessment.

She has worked extensively as a consultant, project designer, and presenter for school systems, regional centers, professional organizations, and state offices of education, and has served as an instructional designer for innovative science curriculum and assessment projects. Recent publications *Eight Essentials of Inquiry-based Science* (2005) and *Becoming a Better Science Teacher: Eight Steps to High Quality and Student Achievement* (2006) were designed as tools to deepen teachers' understandings of standards and standards alignment, and help them meet the demands of implementing inquiry-based science by providing research-based strategies for increasing student achievement.

Her Science Achievement professional development programs for teacher leaders and classroom teachers are individually designed to build leadership capacity and instructional expertise for achieving excellence in science.

PART I

Creating a Vision for Successful Science

On the Shoulders
of Giants

What can we learn from the work of professional scientists that has implications for high quality curriculum and instruction in science education?

DEFINING THE GOAL: SCIENTIFIC LITERACY

We live in a world of science. Simply stated, science is the attempt to uncover and discover the mysteries of the natural world. It is a process of learning and building and revising conceptual understanding over time, often discarding old ideas as new, more plausible ones emerge. The need to know and understanding what "is" and a desire to discover what "might be" motivate humans to seek answers to the continuous flow of questions that arise from the processes of scientific inquiry.

Understanding the natural world and being able to make informed decisions related to the policies and practices that affect the natural world are two characteristics of scientific literacy. Developing such literacy is a lifelong pursuit open to all who wish to participate in the journey. Scientific literacy exists along a continuum where all experiences, both inside and outside of the classroom, slowly move one along to higher levels of learning.

There are many ways to learn about the natural sciences, both formally and informally. Table 1.1 shows some of the environments through which learning can occur.

Much can be learned from informal learning experiences, such as visits to a museum, zoo, nature center, aquarium, planetarium, or other such setting.

Table 1.1   Learning Environments for Science

Informal Learning Environments	Natural Learning Environments
Zoos	Seashores and Tide Pools
Botanic Gardens	Ponds, Lakes, and Shorelines
Museums	Riverbanks and Streambeds
Nature Centers	Mountains
Exploratoriums	Valleys
Aquariums and Oceanariums	Deserts
Planetariums	Fields and Forests
Space Centers	Nature Preserves
Technology Centers	Rain Forests
Amusement Parks	National and State Parks
Manufacturing Plants	School Sites
Weather Stations	Backyards
Airports	
Television/Radio Stations	

Generally, in these environments guides or self-guided maps and information packets are available to describe exhibits and explain natural phenomena.

Natural areas, such as seashores, mountains, deserts, forests, streambeds, parks, school sites, and backyards provide opportunities to explore habitats and observe interactions between living organisms and between living things and nonliving components of their environment. There are no limits to learning environments, but there are limits to learning within those environments.

Limits are imposed by a lack of understanding of how to study science—how to ask questions, make accurate observations, gather and interpret data, and make sense of what is observed. Mediation is an important component of learning, for without it learners are left on their own to make sense of natural phenomena, a practice that can lead to the development of incorrect inferences or misconceptions.

Although curiosity is innate and important for guiding the inquiring mind, scientific literacy must be developed through learning how to:

- make careful observations
- explore natural objects and events
- record and interpret data
- make sense of experiences in the context of science

Scientific literacy requires the learner to go beyond the classroom or laboratory and apply scientific principles to societal issues and life in general. It is important not to lose sight of the ultimate goal of science education: the development of the scientifically literate citizen.

The National Science Education Standards (National Research Council, 1996, p. 22) describes scientific literacy in these ways:

- Scientific literacy means that a person can ask, find, or determine answers to questions derived from curiosity about everyday experiences.
- Scientific literacy means that a person has the ability to describe, explain, and predict natural phenomena.

- Scientific literacy entails being able to read, with understanding, articles about science in the popular press and to engage in social conversation about the validity of the conclusions.
- Scientific literacy implies that a person can identify scientific issues underlying national and local decisions and express positions that are scientifically and technologically informed.
- A literate citizen should be able to evaluate the quality of scientific information on the basis of its source and the methods used to generate it.
- Scientific literacy implies the capacity to pose and evaluate arguments based on evidence and to apply conclusions from such arguments appropriately.
- Individuals display their scientific literacy by appropriately using technical terms and by applying concepts and processes.

Thought and Discussion

1. Review the components of scientific literacy. How are you "scientifically literate"? Identify a spot on the continuum in Figure 1.1 that you believe best represents your level of scientific literacy.

Figure 1.1 Levels of Scientific Literacy

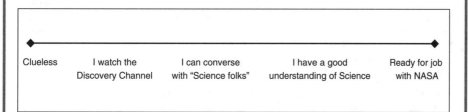

| Clueless | I watch the Discovery Channel | I can converse with "Science folks" | I have a good understanding of Science | Ready for job with NASA |

2. Consider each of the descriptors for scientific literacy. Give examples of when, where, or how the average citizen might apply the skills of scientific literacy in daily life.

3. What do the characteristics of scientific literacy imply about the content, skills, and dispositions students need to function as scientifically literate citizens? What are the implications for curriculum and instruction?

Science for All

One does not have to have a photographic memory or be highly intelligent to become scientifically literate. Science is for all! Curiosity is innate; humans are born with the desire to explore and investigate their environment and understand the world around them.

The learning process is continuous and begins in the early stages of a child's life. Table 1.2 shows a developmental sequence of learning that leads to scientific literacy.

Table 1.2   Sequence of Learning for Scientific Literacy

Stages of Learning	Learning Channels	Learning Experiences That Enhance Science Education
Infancy and Early Childhood	• Development of perception and knowledge through handling objects • Exploration of natural objects and phenomena as motor skills develop • Multisensory experiences	• Early exploration of surroundings and natural objects such as soil, rocks, animals, and plants • Sensory experiences and play influence the development of neurons • Recognition memory aids with familiarity and comfort with natural objects and phenomena
Primary Grades	• Well-designed activities integrating basic science content and process skills with math, reading, and writing • Exposure to natural objects and phenomena • Manipulation of objects and equipment through well-designed activities and experiences	Opportunities to: • master the basic subject matter of life, Earth/space, and physical science through guided or open inquiries • use the basic process skills and vocabulary of science • apply science to their lives • develop dispositions, such as curiosity, honesty, cooperation, and communication skills
Intermediate Grades	• Activities and experiences to develop conceptual knowledge base and skills • Using process and thinking skills and solving problems in the context of science	Continued exposure to: • individual, cooperative, and collaborative approaches to learning • a variety of methods and strategies • many types of equipment and models • resources for reading and extended learning • Use of notebooks for recording and reflection

Middle School	• Activities and experiences to expand learning of basic concepts, processes, thinking skills, and dispositions
	• Opportunities for hypothetical thinking and metacognition
	• Multidimensional thinking; variety and active learning
	• Links to technology and the social world; problem solving
		• Instruction with a focus on:
		  ○ asking questions
		  ○ inquiry-based investigations
		  ○ concept understanding
		  ○ skill development; dispositions
		  ○ reading and writing in context
		  ○ problem solving
		  ○ technology and technological design
		  ○ application of learning
		  ○ history and nature of science
		  ○ careers in science
		• Projects
		• Product development
		• Challenges

High School	• Opportunities to develop deeper understandings of concepts • Continue to develop understanding of and ability to do scientific inquiry • Research and problem solving • Links to technology and society	Further development of concepts and thinking skills as students: • recognize the importance of observations and make sense of the data they collect • link new learning to prior knowledge • apply learning to their lives as well as to community, state, national, and global issues • strengthen understanding of relationships between science and technology

UNDERSTANDING SCIENCE AND HOW SCIENTISTS WORK

All scientific disciplines rely on evidence. The observation of phenomena, formulation of hypotheses, search for evidence, development of theories, and use of logic and reasoning are just a few of many practices that are common throughout the scientific community.

Scientists differ in what they investigate and how they investigate, but their understanding of what constitutes scientifically valid investigations is generally common. Communication between and among scientists is an important aspect of their work.

The search for evidence to support hypotheses and theories requires scientists to be actively involved in investigating and experimenting.

Table 1.3   Types of Observation

Types of Observation	Description
Primary Observation	The validity of scientific claims is determined by data. Firsthand observations and measurements in natural settings and in laboratories provide data.
	To acquire data, scientists use their senses and instruments such as microscopes, probes, and scales to enhance or extend the senses and provide accurate measurements.
Secondary Observation	When firsthand observation is not possible, information is gained through the collection of data recorded by instruments, such as seismograph readings of earthquakes and satellite transmissions of sound and images from outer space.

Investigation

Investigations may involve collections of living and nonliving organisms and materials or collections of data that allow studies of similarities and differences in structure and function, patterns, and changes over time.

Experimentation

In the process of experimenting, scientists control or change one variable at a time to determine the effect of one variable on another or on a condition. All scientific inquiries rely on evidence that is dependent on the quality of instruments, techniques of the researcher, and accuracy of recording and reporting of data.

Thought and Discussion

What Scientists Say About Observation

1. Consider the following three statements about observation. Discuss the implications of these messages for the teaching and learning of K–12 Science.

   - Observation is the absolute basis of all knowledge. The first object, then, in education, must be to lead the child to observe with accuracy; the second, to express with correctness the results of his observation. Johann Heinrich Pestalozzi (1746–1827)

   - Instruction must begin with actual inspection, not with verbal descriptions of things. From such inspection it is that certain knowledge comes. What is actually seen remains faster in the memory than description or enumeration a hundred times as often repeated. John Amos Comenius (1592–1670)

   - Without accurate acquaintance with the visible and tangible properties of things, our conceptions must be erroneous, or inferences fallacious, and our operations unsuccessful. The truths of number, of form, of relationship in position, were all originally drawn from objects; and to present these truths to the child in the concrete is to let him learn them as the race learned them. If we consider it, we shall find that exhaustive observation is an element of all great success. Herbert Spencer (1820–1903)

2. Consider Bacon's description of science. Discuss some implications of his message for classroom instruction.

   Scientific arguments must, ultimately, conform to logical reasoning. Criteria of inference, demonstration, and common sense often determine validity. The principles of logical reasoning that connect evidence and assumptions to conclusions are valued in the scientific community. Formulating tentative hypotheses drives the process of seeking data to support or refute them.

   Only hypotheses that can be put to the test of evidence are useful to scientists. The creativity in science lies in the development of hypotheses and theories and putting them to the test of reality.

   The strongest arguments prove nothing as long as the conclusions are not verified by experience. Experimental science is the queen of sciences and the goal of all speculation. Roger Bacon (1214–1294)

3. How do the quotes about observation and instruction relate to Bacon's description of "scientific arguments"?

SCIENTIFIC DISCOVERIES

Many discoveries have been made by accident. However, generally, a degree of knowledge and/or insight is required to recognize the meaning of the unexpected. Louis Pasteur, whose own career involved serendipity when he accidentally discovered that attenuated microbes can be used for immunization, once noted that "in the field of observation, chance favors only the prepared mind."

The credibility of theories often comes from the scientist's ability to show relationships between seemingly unrelated phenomena. "The essence of science is validation by observation. But it is not enough for scientific theories to fit only the observations that are already known." (Rutherford & Ahlgren, 1990, p. 7)

Theories should have predictive power. The predictions may be about events from the past that are used to construct events in the Earth's history. Prediction is important for the study of processes that occur very slowly, such as mountain building, the life cycles of stars, or the history of the human species.

Bias in the investigator, sample, methods of investigation, or instruments may influence evidence. Scientists must be aware of possible bias in their work. With many different groups of investigators working on a problem, results are less likely to be influenced by bias. Again, communication among scientists is critical to validating results.

In the long run, theories are judged by their results. New or improved versions of theories are often accepted when there is sufficient new evidence to explain more phenomena or answer more questions.

Activity: Defining the Work of Scientists

1. Read the information provided about each of the scientists' theories and/or discoveries. Summarize each scientist's theory or discovery in Table 1.4.

2. Discuss ways the work of scientists can be modeled in the K–12 science classroom.

Table 1.4   Famous Scientists and Their Contributions

Name of Scientist	Theory or Discovery
Nicholas Copernicus	
Marie Curie	
Alfred Wegener	
Jane Goodall	
Wilhelm Roentgen	
Rosalind Franklin	

Nicholas Copernicus (1473–1543)

Around 1514, Copernicus distributed a little handwritten book to a few of his friends who knew that he was the author, even though there was no name on the title page. This book, usually called the *Little Commentary*, set out Copernicus' theory of a universe with the Sun at its center. He based his conclusions on seven axioms that gave several distinct motions to the Earth. No one prior to Copernicus appears to have explained the retrograde motion of the outer planets.

Copernicus was the first person in history to create a complete and general system, combining mathematics, physics, and cosmology. It took the accurate observational work of Brahe, the exhaustive mathematics of Kepler, and the mathematical genius of Newton about 150 years later to take Copernicus' theory as a starting point and glean from it the underlying truths and laws governing celestial mechanics. Copernicus was an important player in the development of these theories, but his work would likely have remained in relative obscurity without the interest of other scientists. To a large extent, Copernicus has achieved a place in history through what amounted to a lucky, albeit shrewd, guess. It is probably more appropriate to view Copernicus' achievements as the first steps toward scientific revolution.

Marie Curie (1867–1934)

Marie Curie was a Polish-French chemist who gave the name "radioactivity" to the emission of radiation from atoms. While working with her husband, Pierre, Marie discovered the radioactive properties of thorium and uranium. She demonstrated that the radioactivity of a substance was proportional to the quantity of radioactive material present.

In 1898, Marie discovered polonium in pitchblende. Later that year, she discovered a trace amount of highly radioactive radium. During the course of four years, the Curies refined eight tons of raw ore to produce one gram of radium.

Marie shared the 1903 Nobel Prize in physics with her husband Pierre and Henri Becquerel for their investigations of radioactivity. She also received another Nobel Prize in 1911 in chemistry for her discovery of two new elements. Madame Curie is one of only four people who have received two Nobel Prizes. Not surprisingly, Marie died of leukemia caused by overexposure to radioactivity.

Alfred Wegener (1880–1930)

Alfred Wegener was a German meteorologist and geophysicist who was one of the first to suggest theories of continental drift and plate tectonics. He suggested that a supercontinent, that he called Pangaea, existed in the past and began to break apart about 200 million years ago.

Pieces of the massive continent drifted slowly (only a few centimeters per year) to their present positions. He noted the fit between South America and Africa, found similarities in ancient climates, and used fossil evidence and similarities of rock structures to support his theory. Wegener's 1915 book was translated into English in 1924, and it aroused hostile criticism. His theory remained controversial until the 1960s, when it became widely accepted. The Continental Drift Theory shows a relationship among such natural phenomena as earthquakes, volcanoes, fossils, shapes of continents, and contours of the ocean floor.

Jane Goodall (1934–)

At the time (1960) when scientists thought that humans were the only species that made and used tools, Jane Goodall observed two chimpanzees strip leaves off twigs and make tools to fish for termites in a nest. Upon learning of Jane's observation, her mentor, Louis Leakey, remarked, "Now we must redefine tool, redefine man, or accept chimpanzees as humans."

During her first year at Gombe, Jane observed chimpanzees hunting and eating bush pigs and other animals. Her observations disproved the previously held theories that chimpanzees were primarily vegetarians and fruit eaters who only occasionally supplemented their diet with insects and small rodents. See http://www.janegoodall.org/jane/index.htmlhttp://hms.d70.k12.il.us/library/naturalists.html for biographical information about naturalists.

Wilhelm Roentgen (1880–1930)

In 1895, Wilhelm Roentgen accidentally discovered a new kind of radiation. He was testing cathode rays to determine if they would pass through glass when he noticed a glow coming from a chemically coated screen a few feet away. Roentgen named the unknown rays "X-rays." He found that X-rays could penetrate some substances but not others. During an experiment, he tested the X-ray absorption of lead. While holding a lead disk to the source of radiation, he exposed his hand to the rays. The shadows that formed on the screen revealed both the impenetrability of lead and the bones in his hand. Roentgen realized that X-rays would penetrate flesh but not bone.

In 1900, he moved to Munich where he became the director of the Institute for Experimental Physics and received the first Nobel Prize for physics the next year.

Information about Roentgen can be found at http://www.uihealthcare.com/depts/medmuseum/galleryexhibits/trailoflight/01discoveryofxray.html and http://www.pa.msu.edu/~brock/d0_homepage/physics-posted/surprise-xrays.html.

Rosalind Franklin (1920–1958)

In April 1953, the journal *Nature* included a statement by Francis Crick and James Watson describing the significance of their discovery of the structure of DNA as a double helix. Their discovery was aided by the research of a young physical chemist named Rosalind Franklin, after Watson was privy (without her knowledge) to one of her X-ray photographs of DNA.

This dedicated British scientist was well known in the scientific community for her study of carbon and later of nucleoproteins and virus structure. A master of X-ray photography, Dr. Franklin photographed the B form of DNA, and her photograph, numbered 51, provided clear evidence to Watson that the molecule was, in fact, a helix, with detectable parameters of tilting and spacing. Watson and Crick received the Nobel Prize in 1962, with little credit given to Dr. Franklin. Later in their careers, Watson and Crick acknowledged that her contribution was critical to the discovery of the double helix of DNA.

SCIENTISTS AS PROBLEM SOLVERS

Scientists engage in laboratory research, but they also engage in field research and problem solving to learn more about how science operates in the natural world. The process of inquiry guides their work. Inquiry is the process through which scientists make observations, acquire data, support their ideas, modify their beliefs, and ask new questions.

Inquiry is defined by the National Science Education Standards (National Research Council, 1996) as:

the diverse ways that scientists study the natural world and propose explanations based on the evidence derived from their work and as the activities used by students to formulate an understanding of the work that scientists do. As a multifaceted activity inquiry involves:

- making observations,
- posing questions,
- accessing and using relevant information,
- planning and carrying out data rich investigations,
- using tools and technology to collect, analyze, and interpret data,
- proposing answers, explanations, and predictions, and
- communicating findings

The inquiry process fosters the use of critical thinking as well as logic and reasoning skills. (p. 23)

Inquiry is the process through which students learn about, understand, and appreciate the work of scientists and develop the knowledge, skills, and dispositions needed to be scientifically literate citizens.

Activity: Inquiry, a Process for Learning and Problem Solving

1. *Inquiry in Problem Solving:* Inquiry is a process that is used in science, but it is also a process that is common to everyday events and problem solving. Table 1.5 shows the components of inquiry. Discuss the components of inquiry. Give some examples of when you might use this process in everyday life and problem solving.

Table 1.5   Components of Inquiry

Making observations; posing questions
Accessing and using relevant information
Formulating hypotheses
Planning and carrying out data rich investigations
Using tools and technology to collect, analyze, and interpret data and to solve problems
Proposing answers, explanations, and predictions; use of logic and reasoning
Communicating findings

2. ***Inquiry in Science—Analyzing Case Studies:*** An analysis of events related to science and technology enables one to see how the components of inquiry are used by working scientists to strengthen their understandings of natural phenomena and to solve problems. Three case studies are presented. They are the types of articles found in the popular press.

- The first case study poses a question by a team of scientists who modify their theories through the comparison of data.
- The second case study describes the work of scientist Marian Diamond.
- The third case study describes how technology was used to solve an environmental problem.

The articles have been analyzed to show the components of inquiry that were utilized in the study. Read the case studies and discuss how each of the stages of inquiry are used in science investigations and problem solving.

Case Study I: Investigating El Niños

Observations: Scientists discovered that the same event can have dramatically different outcomes by observing and comparing the effects of the milder El Niño of 2002–03 and the unusually large El Niño of 1997–98.

Inquiry Question: What might account for different outcomes of similar events? What made one El Niño so much stronger than the other?

Working Hypothesis: Something in the formation of the El Niños caused them to have dramatically different outcomes.

Action: Scientists from the University of Maryland used satellite data of ocean temperatures and sea surface height and computer models to analyze the two events. They noted similarities and differences. They discovered a difference when they studied the waves that were produced by the action of the winds and discovered that a particular kind of wave helped to make one El Niño much stronger and longer lasting than the other.

Findings: The two El Niños started the same way, but when researchers studied ocean height satellite data, they discovered a difference in how the two El Niños developed. Two different types of waves develop during a breakdown in the easterly trade wind system in an El Niño (Kelvin waves and Rossby waves), and these waves cause a change in ocean circulation. When the scientists analyzed satellite data to isolate the effects of the two types of waves, they found that the Kelvin wave component for the two El Niños was similar at first but it strengthened for the 1997 El Niño and weakened for the 2002 El Niño. The influence of the Rossby waves was more striking. These waves had little effect on the development of the 2002 El Niño but contributed greatly to the strength and duration of the 1997 El Niño.

Theory: Currently held theories of El Niño development were changed through the study and data assimilation related to the effects of the two types of waves.

Use of Technology: The research team used satellite data, numerical ocean models, sea surface temperature data from National Oceanic and Atmospheric Administration satellites, and sea surface height measurements from the Topex/Poseidon and Jason satellites, joint missions of NASA and the French space agency.

Next Steps: The study was but one step closer to understanding how an El Niño works and how atmosphere and ocean couple to create a strong event. www.nasa.gov/vision/earth/environment/two-elninos.html

SOURCE: Susan Watanabe, Editor, *FirstGov*, March 14, 2005.

Case Study II: Why Einstein's Brain?

This lecture given by neuroanatomist Dr. Marian Diamond in 1999 highlights a landmark research study in the early 1980s that included samples of Albert Einstein's brain.

Observations: Early research findings showed that the brains from rats living in enriched conditions possessed more glial cells per neuron than brains from rats living in poor conditions. Glial cells and nerve cells are responsible for all of the human behavior generated by the brain.

Inquiry Question: How does the glial cell/neuron ratio in Einstein's brain compare with the glial cell/neuron ratio of other human male brains?

Working Hypothesis: The glial cell/neuron ratio in Einstein's brain is higher than the glial cell/neuron ratio in the brains of other "normal" males.

Action: Dr. Diamond contacted Dr. Thomas Harvey, who was in possession of Einstein's preserved brain since his death. She convinced him to part with four small blocks of Einstein's brain tissue to use in her research. The glial cell/neuron ratio in Einstein's brain would be determined by using a microscope and counting the numbers of cells in the four specimens. Dr. Diamond would then determine the glial cell/neuron ratios in four similar pieces of brain tissue from each of 11 normal males and compare them with the glial cell/neuron ratio found in Einstein's brain.

Findings: The researchers found that in all four areas of the brain, Einstein had more glial cells per neuron than the average male. In only one of the four areas, the left inferior parietal area, did Einstein have significantly more glial cells per neuron.

Theory: The study was just a small, but significant step in brain research by providing additional insight into the relationship between glial cell/neuron ratios and cognitive functions.

Both the inferior parietal and prefrontal association areas of the brain are associated with higher mental functions. These areas associate or analyze information from other areas of the brain. Damage to the inferior parietal regions of the brain results in impairment in writing, spelling, and calculation. At the time of the study, little was known about the degree of specificity in the functions in these zones and additional research was recommended.

Use of Technology/Next Steps: Modern technology such as MRI and PET scans enable researchers to obtain higher resolution images of the brain and learn more about the functions of specific regions.

SOURCE: *Why Einstein's Brain?* A lecture delivered by Dr. Marian Diamond at Doe Library in 1999. Additional information about glial cells, neurons, and the study can be found at New Horizons for Learning: http://www.newhorizons.org/neuro/diamond_einstein.htm.

Case Study III: Cary Finds Innovative Solution to Sludge

Problem: The tremendous growth in population in the city of Cary, NC. has put a demand on the wastewater system and produced excessive amounts of sludge.

Sludge, also called biosolids in the water treatment industry, is the name given to the remains of organisms that digest the solid matter left over after water in sewage has been removed, treated, and released into creeks or reused. In North Carolina, there are strict guidelines for the removal of sludge from wastewater systems. Often operators must contract to have sludge applied to land or removed to landfills.

Solution: A U.S. Representative from North Carolina secured a $1 million grant through the Environmental Protection Agency to help the town build a giant, state-of-the-art dryer that will turn sludge into useful fertilizer. The project will enable the town to manage and utilize the solid waste from the wastewater treatment plants in an "environmentally friendly" manner.

Positive Outcomes: Recycling of waste products for beneficial use; the town may assist nearby communities with similar problems.

Trade-offs: Cost; energy; other

Questions for Research and Discussion:

a. What is sludge? Why is excess sludge a problem? What is generally done with it?
b. What caused the problem in Cary? How was the problem solved?

c. What is a sludge dryer?

d. What are the benefits associated with the use of a sludge dryer? What are the trade-offs?

e. Research how other cities deal with this problem. Do you think the proposed solution is a wise solution to the environmental problem? Why or why not?

f. What is the role of the scientist in problems such as the one cited here? What is the role of technology in helping to solve the problem?

SOURCE: www.house.gov/apps/list/press/nc04_price/020912.sludge.html

Activity: Inquiry, a Process for Investigation and Discovery

Find an article in a newsmagazine, newspaper, or Internet source that describes a scientific investigation, environmental problem, or technological solution.

Create a case study outline similar to those shown, identifying the components of inquiry used in the investigation or problem. Share your case studies.

Describe how you might use this activity to enhance learning about the nature of science in your classroom.

Investigating a Scientist at Work: Following a scientist in the laboratory or in the field provides insights into the nature of the work that they do, the decisions they make, and the myriad of other factors involved in "being a scientist."

Option 1: Analyze a Videotape: Study the work of a contemporary scientist through Bill Kurtis' New Explorer's videotape series or the PBS Scientific American series hosted by Alan Alda. Each episode takes the viewer inside the world of science and follows a scientist doing his or her work in the field. Detailed descriptions of the research of each scientist or crew of scientists are graphically depicted. The successes and failures of each venture are viewed firsthand as the camera crews capture the scientists in action.

Study the questions. As you view the videotape, take notes related to the work of the scientist and complete data in Table 1.6. Discuss your observations and findings.

Option 2: Interview a Scientist: Interview a scientist or "shadow" a scientist for half a day when he or she is involved in a significant component of research. Develop a set of questions that you might ask the scientist to help you to better understand the nature of the work he or she is doing. How has this scientist built upon the work of other scientists? Share your questions and a summary of your findings.

Discuss:

1. What is the significance of knowledge and theories that scientists offer?

2. Summarize: In what ways does the work of scientists, past and present, inform science education and help to define the role of classroom teachers?

Table 1.6   Data Table for Analysis of a Videotape

Questions About the Videotape	Observations and Notes
1. What is the scientist's name and professional title?	
2. Where does this scientist work?	
3. What is his or her branch of science? What does he or she study?	
4. What questions or theories are driving his or her work?	
5. What procedures are being used by the scientist to support his or her theory?	
6. What types of technology are being used by the scientist?	
7. In what ways does this scientist work collaboratively or share work with colleagues from other nations?	
8. How has the research added to the knowledge base of science?	
9. How has this scientist's work contributed to the welfare of humans and other living things on this planet?	
10. What are some of the difficulties or dangers related to this scientist's work?	

THE SCIENTIFIC ENTERPRISE

People from all nations and ethnic backgrounds are engaged in scientific work. Scientists, engineers, mathematicians, physicians, technicians, and others from many fields are involved in the pursuit of the expansion of knowledge or knowledge for practical purposes. Often informal or unexpected influences within a culture determine the direction of scientific research.

For example, recent research of the virus causing Severe Acute Respiratory Syndrome (SARS) was influenced by an outbreak of the deadly disease that had the potential of spreading to millions of people around the world. Scientists isolated four virus samples from the feces and respiratory secretions of civet cats, mammals found in Africa and Asia, and found them to be very similar to the coronavirus found in SARS patients. Before it was brought under control, the disease infected 8,221 people and killed 735 worldwide, according to the World Health Organization.

Research Priorities

Research on diseases that affect large segments of the population, such as heart disease, cancer, and Alzheimer's disease, is often a response to public outcry and/or public and government support. Scientific research is conducted by universities, hospitals, business and industry, government agencies, independent organizations, and scientific associations. Scientists work individually, in small groups, and in large research teams in offices, laboratories, boats, and field stations ranging from outer space to under the sea. They share their findings at professional meetings and publish their work in professional journals. Information technology is an important aspect of research and reporting.

Funding agencies influence the direction of research by providing funds in areas of interest. The federal government of the United States also places restrictions on research that may be dangerous or that may deal with the inhumane treatment of animals or humans used for experimental purposes.

The Ethics of Research

Traditions of accurate recordkeeping, openness, replication of experiments, and critical peer review encourage and support the ethical behavior of scientists. Researchers who have falsified their findings have been severely chastised, and their institutions have lost credibility.

The ethics of science relate to possible harmful effects of applying the results. For example, research on nuclear weapons or germ warfare may have potentially harmful results to humans, but it is not professionally unethical to engage in such research. However, personal ethics may dictate differently. Recently, stem cell research and the practice of cloning have raised some new ethical questions.

Scientists, in the end, are people, just like you and me, doing their jobs and working toward professional goals. Like all professionals, they play two roles: one is the professional role and one is the role of citizen, family member, parent, and so forth. Although they try to eliminate bias in their work, as citizens they may have personal preferences and show support for institutional or community interest groups.

Thought and Discussion

Sometimes scientific research meets ethical issues posed by the general public, such as the one related to the use of human embryos for stem cell research. Consider a statement from the National Institute of Health:

> Stem cells have potential in many different areas of health and medical research. To start with, studying stem cells will help us to understand how they transform into the dazzling array of specialized cells that make us what we are. Some of the most serious medical conditions, such as cancer and birth defects, are due to problems that occur somewhere in this process. A better understanding of normal cell development will allow us to understand and perhaps correct the errors that cause these medical conditions. (stemcells.nih.gov/info/faqs.asp; Healthcare Questions—Stem Cell Information, January 2005)

Discuss:

1. What is the role of K–12 science education in helping students to understand and deal with controversial issues?

2. What are some ways that teachers can deal with these controversial issues in the science classroom?

3. What is the role of the popular press, television, video series, Internet resources, and so forth in promoting an understanding of science and fostering the advancement of science among the general public? What are the strengths of such media? What are the limitations?

Additional Resources:

http://stemcells.nih.gov/info/faqs.asp#whyuse The Official National Institute of Health Resource for stem cell research.

http://stemcless.nih.gov/ A listing of information about stem cells is on the National Institute of Health Web site.

http://www.news.wics.edu/packages/stemcells/ The University of Wisconsin Web site offers information about stem cells written for general audiences.

Activity: Shake, Rock, and Roll

Overview

In this middle/high school level activity, students will simulate the work of a scientist by making observations about objects in closed containers by moving and shaking them. Their observations will provide evidence from which to make inferences about size, shape, and density of objects. Students will understand the nature of science and the importance of making careful observations and inferences to guide thinking and formulate theories when firsthand evidence is not available. The activity would serve as an introduction to the study of the Earth's structure. Additional investigations would be needed to complete the study.

Standards and Key Concepts

The solid Earth is layered with a lithosphere, hot, convecting mantle, and dense metallic core. (NRC, 1996, p. 159)

Grades 5–8: Scientists formulate and test their explanations of nature using observation, experiments, and theoretical and mathematical models. Although all scientific ideas are tentative and subject to change and improvement in principle, for most major ideas in science, there is much experimental and observational confirmation. Those ideas are not likely to change greatly in the future. Scientists do and have changed their ideas about nature when they encounter new experimental evidence that does not match their existing explanations. (NRC, 1996, p. 171)

Grades 9–12: Nature of Scientific Knowledge
- Scientific explanations must meet certain criteria. They must be consistent with experimental and observational evidence about nature, and must make accurate predictions when appropriate, about systems being studied.
- In areas where data or understandings are incomplete, new data may lead to changes in current ideas or resolve current conflicts. (NRC, 1996, p. 201)

Instructional Objectives

Following the completion of this activity, students will:

1. Distinguish between observations and inferences.

2. Describe the role of observation and inference when investigating things that cannot be observed firsthand. Discuss how scientists use observation and inference in formulating theories about the inside of the Earth.

3. Give an example of when they have made observations and inferences when studying science.

4. Explain how scientists use technology to gather evidence and modify theories.

Background Information for the Earth's Structure

The Earth is a closed container with layers of internal material that cannot be observed firsthand by scientists. Seismology has become the principal method of studying the Earth's interior. Almost all we know about the interior of the Earth is based on seismic waves from earthquakes that can be detected worldwide.

Large-scale earthquakes release energy equivalent to almost 2 billion kilograms of high explosives. They kill people and cause enormous amounts of damage to property. They create seismic waves that are sent throughout the Earth's interior and are recorded by observatories around the world. The paths of the seismic waves within the Earth and on the surface provide evidence about the material through which the waves pass. By timing how long waves take to reach various places on the surface of the Earth, scientists can determine whether waves have traveled directly through the Earth or have been bent by passing through dense material.

For example, stations close to the earthquake record P, S, and surface waves in rapid succession; there is more time between arrivals of these waves at stations farther away from the earthquake site.

By studying the paths of seismic waves and the arrival times, seismologists can determine what types of material, solid or liquid, the waves pass through.

Through the analysis of data, seismologists have inferred that the Earth has three distinct layers: a core made up of a solid inner core and a molten outer core, a plastic-like mantle, and a thin crust. The core makes up about 20 percent of the Earth, the mantle makes up about 80 percent, and the crust makes up a mere 1 percent.

The **crust** is the thin outer layer that covers the Earth. The **mantle** lies beneath the crust, 1,800 miles thick (about 3,000 km), and is made of hot rock, so hot that it flows like molasses. The **core** is the metallic center of the Earth. It is hotter than the mantle and thought to be made up of two distinct parts: a 2,200-km-thick liquid outer core (about 1,500 miles) and a 1,250-km-thick solid inner core (about 775 miles thick). As the Earth rotates, the liquid outer core spins, creating the Earth's magnetic field.

The **lithosphere** is composed of the crust and a bit of the upper mantle. The lithosphere extends 60 miles (100 km) below the surface of the Earth.

Within each of the distinct layers are sublayers that have specific properties and features that are worth noting.

Crust: thin, hard rock; floats on the mantle. The crust differs in thickness and age:

Oceanic crust: thinner and younger than the continental crust; about 6 km thick in some places; no rocks older than 200 million years

Continental crust: varies in thickness from 25 to 90 km; some rocks are at least 3.8 billion years old

Rock in both areas has been recycled as a result of geological processes, but the ages differ considerably. The difference in age may be explained by the theory of plate tectonics.

Mohorovicic discontinuity (Moho): the boundary between the crust and the mantle

Upper mantle: in the upper mantle, hot rocks rising from the interior of the Earth melt and form magma; upper mantle is made up of the lithosphere, a rigid layer that extends to a depth of about 100 kilometers, and the asthenosphere, an area less rigid than the lithosphere

Middle mantle: transition zone in which minerals become denser

Lower mantle: area of great pressure

Gutenberg discontinuity: the boundary between the core and the mantle

Outer core: iron and nickel; extreme heat; thought to be permanently molten; currents flowing here may create the Earth's magnetic field

Inner core: heart of the Earth; solid ball of iron and nickel; extreme heat and pressure so great that the core cannot melt

Table 1.7 shows the approximate thickness of the oceanic crust and the continental crust of the Earth, the layer on which you live. Convert "kilometers" to "miles" and determine how thick the Earth's crust is in miles (use 1 km = .62 mi).

Table 1.7   Characteristics of the Earth's Layers

Earth's Layers	Distinguishing Characteristics
Core	Outer core: 2,200 km, mostly molten iron; temperature 3,800°C Inner core: 1,250 km, mostly solid iron with some nickel and cobalt
Mantle	Made up of molten rock made of silicon, oxygen, magnesium, and iron; 3,000 km thick; temperature 1,110°C
Crust	Made up of solid rock, mostly basalt and granite Oceanic crust = "young rock"; about 6 km thick; 1% of Earth Continental crust = 25–90 km thick; older rock Temperature: gets hotter as you get closer to the mantle

The cutaway views in Figure 1.2 show the internal structure of the Earth. The view on the left, drawn to scale, demonstrates that the Earth's crust literally is only skin deep.

The view on the right, not drawn to scale, shows the Earth's three main layers (crust, mantle, and core) in more detail.

Figure 1.2   Views of the Earth's Internal Structure

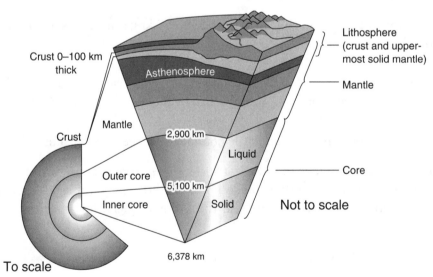

SOURCE: http://pubs.usgs.gov/publications/text/inside.html

Materials and Safety

Per team of two students: One or more small cans or containers with opaque covers (pet treat cans, round cookie containers, small plastic containers)

An assortment of objects with different properties that can be observed by sound or sensation: rubber balls or erasers, plastic cubes, tennis balls, or small objects on wheels; marbles; crayons; blocks or wooden objects; small metal objects; other objects.

Safety: Use only objects that would not be harmful or dangerous.

Inquiry Question

How do scientists learn about natural phenomena when they cannot observe them firsthand, such as when studying the inside of the Earth?

Engagement

Ask students if they have ever observed something—a sound, a smell, a visual observation, a taste, or a tactile observation—but were not able to immediately explain what caused it. Give examples. Ask them to describe what inference(s) they made. Ask and discuss: Were the inferences correct? How did you know? Was there ever a time when you made an observation and never knew for sure what caused it? How did you feel about that?

1. Hold up a closed container and ask students to tell you what is inside.

2. Ask them how they might get information that would help them to know what is inside without actually looking inside the container.

3. Rattle the container. Ask students to describe what they hear. Discuss if the sound provides clues to the contents.

4. Ask students how they think scientists develop theories about things that they cannot directly observe.

Exploration

1. Divide students into teams of two. One member of the team should take one of the containers and put one of the objects inside. The student should not show the partner what is going into the container. Seal the "mystery container."

2. Give the container to the partner. The partner should shake, rock, or roll the container to gather evidence about what is inside.

3. The observer should record what is observed, such as "it sounds like the object is rolling" or "I hear a thud." (Actual observations are sometimes difficult to put into words.)

4. After making several observations, the observer should make an inference (guess based on those observations) about the size, shape, density, or identity of the object and record it. Before showing the observer what is inside the container, the partners should discuss what observations were used to make the inference.

Allow each team member to investigate a closed container with different objects at least twice. Repeat the procedures.

Option: Try the investigation using two of the same objects or two different objects in the container. How do multiple objects affect observations and inferences?

Explanation

Discuss the questions:

1. What did you observe from shaking, rocking, and rolling the container?

2. Describe how the observations led to the inferences you made about the objects inside the container.

3. What kinds of observations do you think scientists make about phenomena they cannot observe firsthand?

4. How would advancement in technology change the theories scientists have about phenomena they cannot observe firsthand? Research some of the ways scientists study the inside of the Earth. What evidence has led to changes in theories about the inside of the Earth?

Elaboration and Extensions

1. Research to discover some ways that scientists learn about natural phenomena when they cannot observe them firsthand, such as the nature of atoms or DNA, the functioning of the human brain, effects of global warming, or objects and conditions in outer space. What types of technology are useful in their quest for understanding?

2. Describe how knowledge and theories have changed over time with the advancement of technology. Trace the history of a theory related to something that cannot be studied firsthand, such as cell theory, theories related to the structure of the planets and other phenomena in outer space, the inside of the Earth, and so forth and identify the role of technology in the various stages of the advancement of that theory.

Evaluation

The first four questions relate directly to the objectives of the investigation. These questions may be answered through notebook entries, interviews, drawings/illustrations, role-play, open response tests, or other authentic measures.

1. Distinguish between observations and inferences.

2. Describe the role of observation and inference when investigating things that cannot be observed firsthand.

3. Give an example of when you have made observations and inferences when studying science.

4. Explain how scientists use technology to gather evidence and modify theories.

5. Optional: Describe some specific ways that scientists learn about natural objects and phenomena when they cannot observe them firsthand, such as what the inside of the Earth is like.

Student Data Sheet for Shake, Rock, and Roll

Inquiry Question:

How do scientists learn about natural phenomena when they cannot observe them firsthand, such as what the inside of the Earth is like?

Prediction:

When firsthand observation is not possible, scientists learn about natural phenomena by:

Table 1.8   Data Table

Trial #	Observations	Inferences
1		
2		
3		
4		

Debriefing Questions

1. What did you observe from shaking, rocking, and rolling the container?

2. Describe how the observations led to the inferences you made about the objects inside the container.

3. What kinds of observations do you think scientists make about phenomena they cannot observe firsthand?

4. How would advancement in technology change the theories scientists have about phenomena they cannot observe firsthand? Research some of the ways scientists study the inside of the Earth.

Thought and Discussion

Analysis of the Activity

1. What is the importance of background information in instructional activities?

2. Revisit the background information for the Shake, Rock, and Roll activity. Read the content information and discuss:

   • In what ways does having the background information enable the teacher to understand the work that scientists do, identify and focus on standards and key concepts, and enrich the learning experience?

   • Give examples of how a rich knowledge base and abundant resources provide ideas for differentiating instruction and helping students relearn the concepts, elaborate on concepts, or extend learning?

Revisit the Initial Question

What can we learn from the work of professional scientists that has implications for high quality curriculum and instruction in science education?

2

Defining
High Quality
Science Teaching

What are the qualities and characteristics of high quality curriculum and instruction?

EXAMINING BELIEFS AND PRACTICES

Science standards reflect the beliefs and practices of the "giants" described in the preceding chapter. Science education is the means through which those beliefs and practices are instilled in the next generation of future scientists and scientifically literate citizens.

Effective teaching and learning begins with a vision for the development of scientifically literate citizens and the acceptance of responsibility for its development. Most states and school systems endorse a set of curricular goals and standards to inform and guide practice focused on the development of scientific literacy.

Generally, beliefs inform practice. However, there are instances where practices do not align with beliefs due to a variety of circumstances. An occasional reflection on beliefs and practices related to the goals of science education and effective science teaching and learning enable teachers to:

- get a snapshot of their learning environments
- think about and consider what they value
- examine reasons for the decisions they make

- celebrate those behaviors they value
- plan ways to more closely align beliefs and practice
- develop action plans for extended learning and professional development

The inventory of beliefs and practices that follows not only enables teachers to identify the state of science education in their classrooms but also helps to shed light on some important aspects of change that may be needed to enhance the overall effectiveness of the science program.

Thought and Discussion

Identifying Beliefs and Practices

1. Use the inventory to identify your beliefs and practices in Science, Math, and Technology Education. Add comments to explain your position or identify new questions.

2. Discuss the questions that follow.

Examining Beliefs and Practices in Science, Math, and Technology Education
For each statement, place a mark on the line to indicate the degree of your beliefs and practices.
0 = least extent and 10 = greatest extent. Record additional comments.

To what extent do you:

1. Focus instruction on a clearly identified set of standards-based key concepts and principles, skills, and dispositions of science found in the state or district curriculum.

   Belief: 0 _____ 10
   Practice: 0 _____ 10
   Comments:

2. Create a context that is meaningful and interesting for students.
   Belief: 0 _____ 10
   Practice: 0 _____ 10
   Comments:

3. Provide flexible grouping patterns for investigations, problem-solving activities, experiments, research, and projects.
   Belief: 0 _____ 10
   Practice: 0 _____ 10
   Comments:

4. Use inquiry, investigation, and firsthand experiences regularly in the science program.
   Belief: 0 _____ 10
   Practice: 0 _____ 10
   Comments:

5. Use equipment and tools to engage learners (calculators, magnifiers and microscopes, balances and mass sets, meter sticks, graduated cylinders, models, computers, etc.)

Belief: 0 _____ 10

Practice: 0 _____ 10

Comments:

6. Provide opportunities for students to collect, record, and make sense of data they generate.

Belief: 0 _____ 10

Practice: 0 _____ 10

Comments:

7. Provide opportunities to reflect on experiences through writing and illustrating.

Belief: 0 _____ 10

Practice: 0 _____ 10

Comments:

8. Provide frequent interaction between students and teacher (and between students) to develop and extend critical and creative thinking, formulate thought, and develop concepts.

Belief: 0 _____ 10

Practice: 0 _____ 10

Comments:

9. Provide opportunities for students to create and share models, graphics, projects, and products.

Belief: 0 _____ 10

Practice: 0 _____ 10

Comments:

10. Model and require students to model valued dispositions, habits of mind, and behaviors.

Belief: 0 _____ 10

Practice: 0 _____ 10

Comments:

11. Use a variety of formative assessment strategies to inform instruction and provide feedback. Give students opportunities to self-assess and monitor their own learning.

Belief: 0 _____ 10

Practice: 0 _____ 10

Comments:

12. Provide opportunities for extended learning and for making connections to technology; to lives of students; to community; to state, national, and world concerns; and to careers.

Belief: 0 _____ 10

Practice: 0 _____ 10

Comments:

(Continued)

(Continued)

Questions for Discussion

1. Describe how beliefs and assumptions affect decisions about classroom instruction and assessment.

2. Give an example of where your beliefs and assumptions determined your decisions about instruction or assessment.

3. Identify one or more practices that you might like to change. What will be required for you to change a practice? Propose an action plan leading to that change.

DEFINING HIGH QUALITY CURRICULUM AND INSTRUCTION: WHAT RESEARCH SAYS

What defines the high quality classroom? Indicators of high quality curriculum and instruction are found throughout the literature. Quality is often described in terms of two separate but connected components of education:

- the systemwide written curriculum
- the instructional approaches that are endorsed by the curriculum

High Quality Curriculum

Throughout this book, the high quality curriculum is defined as a set of learning goals and standards and the programs, equipment, instructional materials, and support that are given to teachers to address them. In addition, two other important elements are necessary in order for the science curriculum at the system level to be high quality.

1. First and foremost, there must be an assessment system to determine the effectiveness of the curriculum and the instructional processes it endorses. This includes more than students' scores on annual standardized tests, since higher order thinking and important skills and dispositions are not always able to be assessed in that way. Further, school district or community-specific goals, goals related to interdisciplinary learning, or those goals related to the applications of learning are not generally assessed through state or national assessments.

2. Second, the high quality curriculum should include ongoing professional development opportunities for teachers that enable them to meet goals and standards on which the curriculum is based. Professional development should address the needs of teachers as they relate to a higher level of performance in the teaching of science.

High Quality Instruction

A set of indicators that define and describe high quality curriculum and instruction have been constructed from reviewing the National Science Education Standards (NRC, 1996), the Benchmarks for Science Literacy (AAAS, 1993), and the literature and research in effective teaching. Three resources are shown that offer overlapping and consistent descriptions of "high quality."

1. Carol Tomlinson (1999, 2004) offers indicators of high quality instruction in her description of academic diversity. She identified factors that assist teachers in providing for diverse populations of students. Among the indicators of high quality curriculum and instruction are:

   o There is a focus on essential knowledge, understandings, and skills valued by professionals in the field.

   o Curriculum and instruction are organized, unified, and sensible to the student.

   o Student misconceptions are addressed.

   o Instruction enables students to participate in respectful work.

   o Students are able to use the learning in important ways.

   o Instruction includes cognition and metacognition.

   o Instruction and assessment are inseparable.

   o Students generate knowledge.

2. The Study of K–12 Mathematics and Science Education in the United States conducted by Horizon Research, Inc. (Weiss et al., 2003) identified indicators of effective lessons. In this study, high quality lessons:

   o Engaged students with mathematics and science content

   o Created an environment conducive to learning

   o Ensured access for all students

   o Used questioning to monitor and promote understanding

   o Helped students make sense of the mathematics/science content

The research reported that, although teachers seem to know and be comfortable with the content of their lessons, the nation's classrooms fall short of providing high quality mathematics and science education for all students. Intellectual rigor, opportunities for creating meaning, and good use of questions for the development of concepts and skills are just a few of the important components that were found to be missing from classroom instruction.

3. James Stronge (2002) defines effective teaching as a product of good classroom management, organization, effective planning, and a teacher's personal characteristics. He points to the importance of the presentation of material and the student's ability to make authentic connections to it. He further identifies the behaviors of effective teachers, which include:

o Use of student questions to guide lessons

o Use of strategies to promote higher order thinking

o Use of a variety of activities and strategies to engage students

o Monitoring of student engagement in all activities

o Maintaining a student-centered classroom

o Providing feedback

o Designing assignments based on objectives

o Implementing elements of effective lessons

INDICATORS OF HIGH QUALITY TEACHING

Based on the messages found throughout the National Science Education Standards and the Benchmarks for Science Literacy and supported by research in effective teaching and learning, eight indicators of high quality teaching have been identified in Figure 2.1 to guide the curriculum development and implementation process described in the model for successful science.

The indicators of high quality teaching provide a framework for addressing the content standards for which teachers will be held accountable and for providing a rich program of activities and experiences to maximize learning. Thus, the indicators of high quality are a powerful resource for the design or modification of instructional materials—units of instruction and the activities and experiences that encompass it—that may be used to guide the teaching process.

Figure 2.1 Eight Indicators of High Quality Teaching

High Quality Teaching:

Addresses clear and appropriate learning goals

Builds concepts and principles, develops skills, and practices dispositions valued by the scientific community

Accommodates diversity through meaningful contexts

Includes varied methods that engage and challenge students intellectually and address prior learning, misconceptions, and new learning

Embeds strategies that allow students to develop new or modified thinking frames with links to their own lives, technology, and issues relevant to their community, state, nation, and world

Develops thinking and problem-solving skills by using questioning, reflection, applications, graphic organizers, and other strategies that help students to make sense of what they are learning

Incorporates a well-designed assessment system to monitor and guide the learning process and to provide frequent feedback to students about their learning

Utilizes equipment, materials, and resources for enhancing learning and providing a challenging learning environment

PEDAGOGICAL CONTENT KNOWLEDGE FOR SUCCESS

Identifying the indicators of high quality teaching is only the first step in teaching science successfully. High quality teaching must be linked to the context of science in ways that reflect how science operates in the professional world. Much has been written about the difference between content knowledge and pedagogical content knowledge in relation to effective teaching and learning in a subject area.

> The content knowledge necessary for expertise in a discipline needs to be differentiated from the pedagogical content knowledge that underlies effective teaching. (Redish, 1996; Shulman, 1986, 1987, in NRC, 2000)

Shulman (1986) makes it clear that pedagogical content knowledge is not equivalent to knowledge of a content domain plus a generic set of teaching strategies.

Pedagogical content knowledge may be defined as a set of teaching strategies that are strongly connected to ways of knowing, thinking, and learning within the discipline and operationally may be defined in terms of what an effective science teacher needs to know and be able to do.

In his study, Ermeling (2005) used a systematic approach to professional development and the development of pedagogical content knowledge that enabled teachers to adopt a research-based strategy and to implement the strategy in their teaching of scientific concepts. The project involved teachers in twenty hours of work over four months and found that through the process teachers were able to personalize and refine the strategies in their content areas.

Thus, pedagogical content knowledge can be defined operationally as a set of behaviors exhibited by effective teachers in the classroom. Some of these behaviors are listed in Table 2.1. There is a depth of understanding of the teaching/learning process that is implied in this description of effective teachers.

The model frameworks provided in this book for the design and development of high quality instructional materials focus on important goals and standards of the discipline and challenge teachers to use a variety of research-based methods and strategies that are most effective for reaching those goals and standards. The design process provides a set of blueprints that can be used to inform and guide effective classroom practice.

A FRAMEWORK FOR INSTRUCTIONAL MATERIALS

Instructional materials can be powerful tools for providing high quality instruction in the science classroom. Well-designed units and carefully crafted lessons may be used to guide the instructional process for all teachers, but especially beginning or ill-prepared teachers.

Table 2.1   Behaviors of Effective Teachers

Effective Teachers of Science
• Know the structure of their discipline and are able to use it to guide assignments and assessments
• Select appropriate strategies and questions throughout the instructional process
• Know the difficulties that students are likely to face
• Address prior knowledge and misconceptions
• Understand students' ways of knowing and thinking
• Know how to link prior knowledge with new knowledge to make learning meaningful and build deeper understanding of concepts and principles
• Know how to assess student progress and use assessment as a learning tool
• Know how to prescribe appropriate channels for relearning or extended learning

The unit development process presented in Chapters 3–8 has been used successfully by thousands of preservice and in-service teachers to develop high quality, standards-based products. The process aligns with the indicators of high quality teaching not only to operationally define each indicator, but to highlight the importance of each to the teaching/learning process.

The correlation of indicators with steps shown in Table 2.2 provides a vision for the development of high quality curricular materials. Each of the eight steps is described in detail in Chapters 3–8.

Table 2.2   Eight Steps to High Quality Teaching

Chapter	**Indicators of High Quality Teaching**	**Steps for Developing High Quality Units and Lessons**
3	**Steps One–Three** Address clear and appropriate learning goals Build concepts and principles Develop skills and practices dispositions valued by the scientific community	**Steps One–Three** 1. Select a topic or theme from the state or local framework for science education for your grade level. Research and review content information about the topic 2. Select a set of key concepts and principles appropriate for the grade level around which the unit will be developed.

Chapter	Indicators of High Quality Teaching	Steps for Developing High Quality Units and Lessons
		• Design one or more graphic organizers to show relationships between concepts or concept categories for the unit. 3. Consider process skills of science, critical and creative thinking skills, and dispositions to include and emphasize.
4	**Step Four** Accommodates diversity through meaningful contexts	**Step Four** Create a context for meaningful learning. • Consider various types of contexts for the development of high quality instruction. • A sample unit in a cultural context is included.
5	**Step Five** Includes varied methods that engage and challenge students intellectually and address prior learning, misconceptions, and new learning Embeds strategies that allow students to develop new or modified thinking frames with links to their own lives, technology, and issues relevant to their community, state, nation, and world	**Step Five** Research learning activities and experiences. Modify existing activities or design new activities. • Use a consistent format for crafting each instructional activity and experience. • Include multiple and varied methods and strategies for meeting the needs of learners. • Consider activities and experiences for relearning and for extended learning.
6	**Step Six** Develops thinking and problem-solving skills by using questioning and other strategies for students to make sense of what they are learning	**Step Six** Include a variety of ways for students to frame thought, link new learning to prior learning, and make connections to their lives, technology, and society. • Develop a student notebook that reflects what students will design, do, record, write, research, and so forth throughout the unit. • Frame thought and show understanding and meaning through visuals, performances, products, and so forth.

(Continued)

Table 2.2 (Continued)

Chapter	Indicators of High Quality Teaching	Steps for Developing High Quality Units and Lessons
7	**Step Seven** Incorporates a well-designed assessment system to monitor and guide the learning process and to provide frequent feedback to students about their learning	**Step Seven** Design a rich assortment of formative assessments. • Establish rubrics to enable students to self-assess. • Use assessment data to assess effectiveness of unit.
8	**Step Eight** Utilizes equipment, materials, and resources for enhancing learning and providing a challenging learning environment	**Step Eight** Consider resources, equipment, and materials that will be needed for effective instruction. Consider management strategies and safety issues.

ACTION PLANS

Two (or more) action plans may be considered to guide unit development or modification. Both plans align instruction and classroom assessment with standards and standardized tests, but they go about the process in slightly different ways.

- **Action Plan #1:** If assessments are not predetermined, the ideal design sequence might be:
  1. Identify standards and instructional goals; select a topic or theme; research content and identify key concepts around which the unit will be developed.
  2. Design multiple and varied assessments that align with standards and goals. Consider a variety of ways for students to show that they have met the standards throughout the instructional process.
  3. Decide the context. Identify inquiry activities, experiences, and resources to teach the important messages of the standards and address instructional goals. Use a variety of methods, strategies, and best practices to meet the needs of all learners.

When content is unfamiliar, teachers may prefer to reverse steps two and three and consider assessments after they have become more familiar with the content.

- **Action Plan #2:** "Working Backwards" approach—if assessments are already in place, the order of curriculum development or modification might be:

   1. Study the types of assessments that are used to determine what students know and are able to do. Link the concepts and skills addressed in the assessments to district goals and standards to get an understanding of how standards are interpreted.

   2. Consider the high priority goals and standards of your curriculum. Identify topics/themes, resources, inquiry activities, and experiences that address them. Create a rich environment for learning that will enable students to develop deep understandings of concepts and ability to perform skills so they are prepared adequately to deal with standards-based assessments.

This plan may be thought of as "teaching to the test," but it is, in fact, teaching to the standards on which test items are based. The standards are the focus of instruction, not the test items. When assessments are aligned with standards, the teacher is free to be creative and clever in the design of instruction that addresses the key concepts and skills.

Thought and Discussion

1. Describe the differences in the two approaches to curriculum development.

2. What are some other approaches or modifications to these approaches that might be used to achieve the same goal?

Revisit the Initial Question

What are the qualities and characteristics of high quality curriculum and instruction?

PART II

Giant Steps to High Quality Teaching

The Role of Science Standards

Indicators of High Quality Teaching

High Quality Teaching:

- Addresses clear and appropriate learning goals
- Builds concepts and principles, develops skills, and practices dispositions valued by the scientific community

Building High Quality Materials to Inform High Quality Instruction

Steps One–Three:

- Select a topic or theme from the state or local framework for science education for your grade level. Research and review content information about the topic.
- Select a set of key concepts and principles appropriate for the grade level around which the unit will be developed. Design one or more graphic organizers to show relationships between concepts or concept categories for the unit.
- Consider process skills of science, critical and creative thinking skills, and dispositions to include and emphasize.

How do standards clarify learning goals and inform the teaching/ learning process?

UNDERSTANDING STANDARDS

National and state standards projects describe what students should know and be able to do at various grade levels throughout a K–12 science program. These projects describe unifying concepts and processes and essential goals from life, Earth and space, and physical sciences, as well from the following standards:

- Science as Inquiry
- Science and Technology
- Science in Personal and Social Perspectives
- History of Science
- Nature of Science

These five standards are often viewed as strands that interact with or "flow through" the life, Earth and space, and physical sciences standards to provide a rich approach to the development of scientific literacy. Figure 3.1 provides a vision for the way these standards relate to the content standards of life, Earth and space, and physical sciences and should be addressed in a science program.

Figure 3.1   The Integration of Science Standards

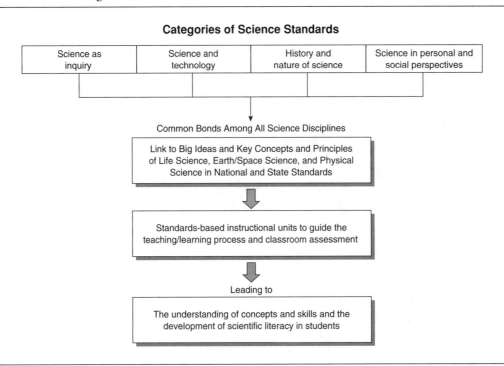

┌───┐

Thought and Discussion

What do the standards look like? Use a national, state, or local standards document for science education.

1. Identify how each of these standards is represented in the document.
   - Science as Inquiry
   - Science and Technology
   - Science in Personal and Social Perspectives
   - History of Science
   - Nature of Science

2. Identify the unifying concepts and processes that are described in the document. Note that all the disciplines of science—life, Earth and space, and physical sciences—fall under the same unifying concepts and processes.

3. How are the content standards presented? Identify key concepts and principles (sometimes called benchmarks) for life, Earth and space, and physical sciences.

4. Mapping a framework for K–12 science, that is, defining and sequencing the standards, topics, or themes and clarifying instructional goals for each grade level, is often done at the state or local level to ensure that:
   - all important standards, topics, or themes are addressed,
   - there is a plan for building conceptual understanding in the K–12 sequence, and
   - there is ownership for content at each grade level.

Identify the topics, themes, and goals for your grade level.

└───┘

IDENTIFYING AND UNPACKING POWER STANDARDS

The standards for the life, Earth and space, and physical sciences and their variations are often written to provide freedom and flexibility in the ways content will be addressed in the classroom. The vast amount of content in the natural sciences is both a blessing and a curse since there are many interesting and exciting topics and themes through which to address the standards. It is overwhelming to attempt to give all of the standards equal time and energy.

Identifying "power standards" and "unpacking" those standards to identify important big ideas are two popular approaches to selecting and managing content for instructional units.

Identifying Power Standards

In some state and local standards documents, high priority standards are identified. Standards that are of highest priority are generally those considered to be important to understanding the nature of science or those dealing with state or local natural phenomena. High priority standards are often assessed annually at the state level and found on standardized tests.

Unpacking the Standards

This term implies a process through which standards are analyzed to identify the important messages that are then synthesized into meaningful and manageable chunks of information. Through discussion, important key concepts, concept categories, relationships among concepts, skills, applications, and the like are identified, and these become the focus for classroom instruction.

Synthesizing the standards into big ideas or chunks of information also makes it possible to provide greater depth of study in the classroom. The "less is more" approach that results implies that with more time devoted to fewer topics, the learner will:

- achieve a greater depth of understanding of concepts and processes
- more likely be involved in an inquiry-based approach to learning
- be able to link science to technology and social and personal perspectives
- discover the human side of science, which includes the historical aspects and the nature of the discipline

---

Thought and Discussion

1. Identify the high priority standards in your state or local standards document. Suggest and discuss reasons why these standards are considered to be important or why they might be assessed annually on standardized tests.

2. Select one of the content standards at your grade level or grade level span. In small groups, analyze that standard and the subcategories under the standard. Unpack that standard. Identify the most important messages and big ideas that relate to that standard. Share your ideas.

Table 3.1   Unpacking the Standards

Standard	Big Ideas (key concepts and principles)
	✓
	✓
	✓
	✓

CONCEPTS, SKILLS, AND DISPOSITIONS IN A SCIENCE FRAMEWORK

Topics and themes in a structural framework identify the context through which important standards will be addressed. Common topics and themes for K–4 Science are shown in Table 3.2, common topics and themes for 5–8 Science are shown in Table 3.3, and common topics and themes for 9–12 Science are shown in Table 3.4.

Table 3.2   Topics and Themes for K–4 Science

Content Standard	Topics and Themes
Physical Science and Technology	• properties of matter • position and motion of objects • water; sink and float • machines and motion • light, sound, heat, and other energy sources • magnetism and electricity • distinguish between natural objects and human-made objects • natural resources
Life Science	• characteristics of organisms • life cycles: eggs to chick; seed to plant • structure/function of plants • butterflies, insects, and spiders • the senses • the environment • mammals and other animal groups • plants • life cycles of animals and plants • introduction to human body systems • health and nutrition • plant and animal habitats such as the rain forest, desert, or forest • extinct animals such as dinosaurs or other animal group of interest
Earth and Space Science	• properties of Earth materials • Earth structure • composition of soil • rocks and fossils • introduction to volcanoes and earthquakes • objects in the sky: investigating space; solar system; Sun, Earth, and Moon system; investigating shadows • cycles of day/night and seasons • air, water, and weather • pollution • recycling

Table 3.3   Topics and Themes for 5–8 Science

Content Standard	Topic and Themes
Physical Science and Technology	• properties of matter and subatomic particles • properties of water; density and buoyancy; the water cycle • changes in properties of matter: physical and chemical changes • magnets and motors, simple machines, complex machines • forces and motion: aerodynamics; amusement park physics • inventions • energy and transfer of energy—electricity, solar, nuclear, light, sound, heat, etc. • applications of science to technology
Life Science	• structure and function in living systems: cells, tissues, organs, and organisms • single-cell and microscopic organisms; animal groups • human body systems and health • reproduction and heredity: genetics and heredity; Human Genome Project • regulation and behavior: viruses/bacteria and diseases; affects of tobacco and alcohol on the human body • populations • ecology and ecosystems • diversity and adaptations in plants and animals • plant and animal behavior • evolution
Earth and Space Science	• Earth systems: structure of the Earth; Earth's forces • Earth history; historical geology • theories of plate tectonics and sea floor spreading • oceanography and structure of the ocean basins • weather systems • forces: erosion; folding and faulting • rocks, minerals, and fossils • soil science • volcanoes, earthquakes, and tsunami • water and the water cycle • environments and natural hazards • Earth in the solar system; systems in space

Table 3.4   Topics and Themes for 9–12 Science

Content Standard	Topics and Themes
Physical Science and Technology	• structure of atoms • structure and properties of matter; atomic and subatomic particles • chemical reactions • motions and forces: amusement park physics; active physics; physics of sport • conservation of energy and increase in disorder • interactions of energy and matter • the role of technology in local, national, and global societies
Life Science	• the cell • molecular basis of heredity • biological evolution • interdependence of organisms • matter, energy, and organization in living systems • behavior of organisms • population dynamics • personal and community health issues
Earth and Space Science	• energy in the Earth system • geochemical cycles • origin and evolution of Earth system • origin and evolution of the universe • natural resources • environmental quality • natural and human-induced hazards

K–12 Framework for Science

A framework is often used to provide a visual of topics and to show the ways content understanding develops over time. Often units of instruction are designed in life, Earth and space, and physical sciences (and sometimes health) for each grade level. Table 3.5 shows a framework for K–12 Science.

⌐ **Thought and Discussion** ⎯⎯⎯⎯⎯⎯⎯⎯

1. Analyze the sample framework in Table 3.5 and identify any patterns you see related to big ideas and concept development.

2. What other observations can you make about the framework?

3. Compare the framework with one from your state or school system. Describe how the framework is similar to and different from the one you are analyzing.

Table 3.5   A Sample K–12 Curriculum Framework by Topics

Grade	Life Science	Earth and Space Science	Physical Science
K	The senses; pets; living things around me	Weather; Sun and Moon; making observations	Water; sink and float; properties of objects
1	Egg to chick; structure of seeds; serial ordering	Day/night and seasons; change in Earth and sky; predictions	Energy: light; sound; heat
2	Butterfly life cycle; spiders and insects; seed to plant	Solar system; Sun, Moon, Earth system; identifying relationships	Properties of matter—solid, liquid, gas; classification
3	Structures of plants and animals and their functions; classification of plants and animals	Rocks, minerals, and fossils; measurement and time	Introduction to force and motion; introduction to magnetism and electricity; making inferences
4	Plants, animals, and physical components of the rain forest or other ecosystems; transfer of energy in a system	Earth in space; Earth structure; Earth forces; components of systems	Mystery powders—matter: physical/chemical change; inferences; cause/effect
5	Habitats; plant/animal relationships and behavior; introduction to the microscope; single-cell organisms; adaptation; hypothesis testing	Weather and weather forecasting; prediction Hydrosphere: water and the water cycle	Properties of water: density, buoyancy, surface tension, etc.; molecular structure of water; evidence
6	Cells; structure and function in living systems; cell division; applications to technology and society	Rocks and minerals; rock/soil cycle; historical geology—change over time	Magnetism and electricity; measurement and graphing; aerodynamics; technology; history of science
7	Diversity and adaptation; populations and ecosystems; adaptations and extinctions; transfer of energy in living systems	Lithosphere: dynamic Earth; Earth's forces—volcanoes and earthquakes, etc.; weathering and erosion; folding/faulting; constancy and change	Forces and motion; energy and transfer of energy—light and color, sound, heat, nuclear, solar, etc; hypothesis testing
8	Reproduction and heredity; human anatomy and physiology; Human Genome Project	Astronomy; universe and space exploration; atmosphere	Properties and changes of properties in matter; subatomic particles; inventions
9–12	Cell theory: structure and function; DNA and molecular basis of heredity; evolution and natural selection; interactions in the biosphere; matter, energy, and organization in living systems; behavior of organisms; history of science; applications and ethics	Understanding the science in the community; the Earth's system: energy and transfer of energy, cycles, and climate, origin and evolution; the universe: origin and evolution; evidence and changes of evidence for theories	Atomic theory; Periodic Table; chemical bonds; molecular models; chemical reactions; Newton's Laws of Motion; forces in nature; energy transfer and conservation; interactions between energy and matter; nature of scientific evidence

CONCEPTS AND PRINCIPLES

Fundamental concepts and principles are statements of what students should know and be able to do. They describe what is to be learned about the topic at a particular grade level or within a grade level span. The National Science Education Standards (NRC, 1996) and the Benchmarks for Science Literacy (AAAS, 1993) offer fundamental concepts and principles for the content standards.

For example, the NSES K–4 Standard **The Life Cycle of Organisms** has three concepts.

- The first concept describes that plants and animals have life cycles with stages from birth to death and that life cycles are different for different organisms.
- The second concept focuses on the resemblances of plants and animals to their parents.
- The third concept deals with differences between inherited traits and acquired traits.

Similar concepts are included in Benchmarks for Science Literacy under the headings **Flow of Matter and Energy** and **The Human Organism**.

At the 5–8 level, the number of concepts and principles is greater, and they build on the understandings that were established at the K–4 level. The NSES Standard **Earth in the Solar System** has four fundamental concepts dealing with:

- the components of the solar system
- the motion of objects in the solar system
- gravity as the force that governs the system
- the importance of the Sun as the major source of energy for the system

Similar concepts are described in Benchmarks under the headings **The Universe** and **The Earth.**

The standards at the 9–12 level take the concepts from the 5–8 level to new levels of understanding that include both depth of content and understanding of relationships. At the 9–12 level, there is an emphasis on the intradisciplinary nature of science.

STANDARDS INFORM INSTRUCTION

State standards documents are often based on the important messages of the national standards projects and include similar concepts and principles around which inquiry-based units can be developed.

Example 1

The descriptive map in Figure 3.2 shows a set of key concepts for an intermediate or middle grade unit on the Properties of Water.

Figure 3.2   Concepts for a Unit on Properties of Water

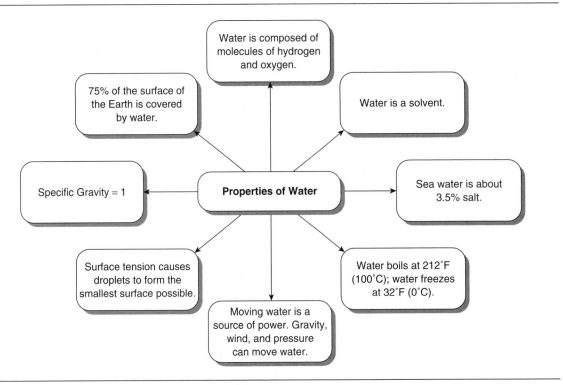

Example 2

A unit in Earth Science at the middle grade level might be developed around these key concepts:

1. Students will describe the features of the Earth and the processes that shape the Earth including:

   - major layers of the Earth
   - processes that create geologic features such as folding, faulting, volcanism, and sedimentation
   - realization that the processes are continually shaping the Earth (erosion, weathering, plate tectonics) just as they have throughout geologic history

2. Students will explain the rock cycle and describe how it affected the formation of rock in their state. They will describe both slow changes, such as weathering, and rapid changes, such as landslides and earthquakes, in the Earth's surface.

3. Students will describe theories of fossil formation and identify plants and animals living today that are similar to fossil forms.

Example 3

A unit in physical science dealing with Force and Motion at the high school level might be developed around these topics:

- Galileo's Principle of Inertia
- Newton's Laws of Motion
- Center of mass
- Gravity as universal force
- Friction between different surfaces
- Momentum and conservation of momentum
- Centripetal acceleration and force

Once standards-related key concepts are identified, a rich assortment of inquiry-based investigations and meaningful experiences are needed to guide the teaching/learning process.

It is imperative that the key concepts that are the focus of instruction are clearly identified and defined from a variety of references, experiences, and resources at the student level of understanding and beyond. Examples of key concepts for a few common topics are shown in Table 3.6.

Through a well-developed K–12 program and high quality instruction, students will be able to relate to prior knowledge and experiences as they build deeper, richer concept understandings and develop the skills of inquiry.

Thought and Discussion

1. Refer to the previous activity where you analyzed one of the standards for your grade level. Identify the themes or topics that were apparent.

2. Identify key concepts and principles that relate to that standard. Discuss these as the basis for activities and experiences. Refer to the examples in Table 3.6.

Table 3.6   Unit Topics and Related Concepts

Unit Topics	Related Concepts
Ecosystems	The biosphere includes all the Earth's environments, the oceans and water areas, the air, and the landmasses.
	Ecologists study the ways living things interact with each other and with the abiotic factors such as sunlight, air, water, minerals, wind, and soil.
	Organisms in ecosystems exchange energy and nutrients among themselves and with the environment.
Earth in Space	Galaxies are clusters of billions of stars and may have different shapes; galaxies cannot be seen with the unaided eye because of their vast distance from Earth.
	Gravitational attraction between all forms of matter holds objects on the Earth, causes tides, keeps the solar system and galaxies together, and controls the movement of the planets in the solar system.

(Continued)

Table 3.6 (Continued)

Unit Topics	Related Concepts
Weather	Astronomical units and light years are measures of distance between the Sun, stars, and the Earth. The atmosphere is a mixture of gases, and it has properties that can be measured and used to predict changes in weather and to identify climatic patterns. Predicting or forecasting weather involves observing and analyzing the relationships between the Earth's physical features and atmosphere and the amount of energy supplied by the Sun. Temperature, humidity, air pressure, and wind direction and speed influence weather.

A PLANNING GUIDE FOR INSTRUCTION

Table 3.7 shows a planning guide for a standards-based unit on Cell Theory for the middle school level. The column on the left identifies standards or content categories, such as Basic Needs of Cells, Structure and Function, Cell Division, and so forth, and the middle column identifies important concepts that might be included in a unit of instruction to address the standards.

The key concepts become the focus for the activities, investigations, and experiences in the unit. Activities and experiences that address the key concepts should be added to the column at the right.

Table 3.7   Planning Guide for Instruction

Standards/Content Categories	Key Concepts	Activities, Investigations, and Experiences
History of Cell Theory Throughout history scientists have made discoveries that have added to the wealth of knowledge about cells.	**Cell Theory** The cell is the smallest unit of life. All life forms are made from one or more cells. Cells only arise from preexisting cells 1. Scientists associated with cell theory: • Robert Hooke (1635–1703) coined the term "cells" for the tiny, hollow structures in thin slices of cork he observed through a compound microscope. • Anton van Leeuwenhoek • Matthias Scheiden • Theodor Schwann • Rudolph Virchow	

Standards/Content Categories	Key Concepts	Activities, Investigations, and Experiences
Basic Needs Cells, like organisms, need food, water, and air; a way to dispose of waste; an environment in which to live. All living things are composed of cells, from just one to many millions, whose details are usually visible only through a microscope. Within cells, many of the basic functions of organisms (energy, food, getting rid of waste) are carried out. The way in which cells function is similar in all living organisms.	2. All organisms (except bacteria) are composed of one or more eukaryotic cells. Bacteria (Monera) are smaller and simpler in internal structure and are prokaryotic cells. 3. The cell is the smallest unit in the living organism that is capable of integrating the essential life processes. 4. Properties of cells: cells store information in genes made of DNA; they use proteins as their main structural material; they synthesize proteins in ribosomes; they are enclosed by a cell membrane.	
Cell Differentiation Different body tissues and organs are made up of different kinds of cells. Various organs and tissues function to serve the needs of all cells for food, air, and waste removal. Cells repeatedly divide to make more cells for growth and repair. The same genetic information is copied in each cell of the new organism.	5. Cells carry on the functions needed to sustain life. They grow and divide, thereby producing more cells. Cells take in nutrients, which they use to provide energy for the work they do and to make the materials that cells or organisms need.	
Cell Division: Mitosis and Meiosis; Heredity and Reproduction The fertilized egg cell, carrying genetic information from each parent, multiplies to form the complete organism. Following fertilization, cell division produces a small cluster of cells that then	6. Mitosis is the process by which living things make new cells. 7. The two new cells produced through mitosis are identical to the original and to each other. 8. Meiosis is a reduction division, which means that the amount of genetic material in the cell splits in two and remains separated until fertilization occurs. Egg and sperm cells carry only half the amount of genetic material as other types of cells.	

(Continued)

Table 3.7 (Continued)

Standards/Content Categories	Key Concepts	Activities, Investigations, and Experiences
differentiate by appearance and function to form the basic tissues of an embryo.	9. During meiosis a parent cell divides two times, leading to the formation of four cells. These cells have one of each of the pairs of chromosomes of the parent cell.	
Body's Defense System The length and quality of human life are influenced by many factors, including sanitation, diet, medical care, sex, genes, environmental conditions, and personal health behaviors. White blood cells engulf invaders or produce antibodies that attack them. Vaccines induce the body to build immunity to a disease without actually causing the disease itself. Specific kinds of germs cause specific diseases, viruses, bacteria, fungi, and parasites that may infect the human body and interfere with normal body functions.	10. Environmental conditions such as pollen, gases, and other air pollutants, chemicals, and other water and land pollutants can seriously affect health. 11. Viruses, bacteria, and parasites cause diseases and illnesses that affect the quality and length of human life. 12. Additional Research Topics: • Health issues related to cells • Diseases of the human body • DNA and forensic science • Human Genome Project • Genetic engineering • Role of technology in cell theory	

Thought and Discussion

1. Identify some rich activities, investigations, or experiences that address the key concepts for cell theory or use the planning guide to create a unit outline for a content area with which you are familiar.

2. Study the relationship between standards, key concepts, and activities. Discuss the importance of selecting activities, investigations, and experiences that address learning styles, multiple intelligences, and diversity and allow for differentiation of instruction to meet the needs and interests of students.

INTERDISCIPLINARY UNITS

Topics and themes often provide opportunities for interdisciplinary study. There are many benefits to this approach. Among them are opportunities to:

- provide depth of content and development of process, thinking, and creative skills across disciplines
- address a broad range of multiple intelligences
- allow students to show concept understanding in unique and personal ways

To be successful, interdisciplinary units must address important concepts and skills from all the disciplines that will be included. This means that the developer must select important concepts and skills from the state or local standards or curriculum guide for each subject area and be able to specifically address them through the activities and experiences in the unit.

For example, to integrate language arts, students may compose a written response to a letter inviting them to conduct an investigation using correct form, grammar, and spelling. They may be a part of a research team requiring them to develop an impact study or a lab report. The assignment should be structured to meet one or more instructional goals for language arts.

DESIGNING AN INTERDISCIPLINARY UNIT

An interdisciplinary approach broadens the scope of the topic and provides opportunities for students to learn concepts and skills in many ways that tie to the array of intelligences they innately have.

In developing an interdisciplinary unit, consideration must first be given to the instructional goals and key concepts from each discipline. Then activities can be crafted with a focus that deepens student understanding of the concepts, practices the skills and dispositions valued by the educational community, and results in meaningful learning.

One approach to developing an interdisciplinary unit is to brainstorm a list of possible activities that relate to the topic and instructional goals for a variety of content areas. The descriptive map in Figure 3.3 shows a list of instructional activities from several disciplines for a primary grade unit on Spiders and Insects.

PROCESS SKILLS AND DISPOSITIONS

The use of process and thinking skills and the practice of valued dispositions are closely linked to standards and instructional goals. Throughout the inquiry process, the process skills and dispositions should be used as the vocabulary of

Figure 3.3   Planning Map for an Interdisciplinary Unit on Spiders and Insects at the Primary Level

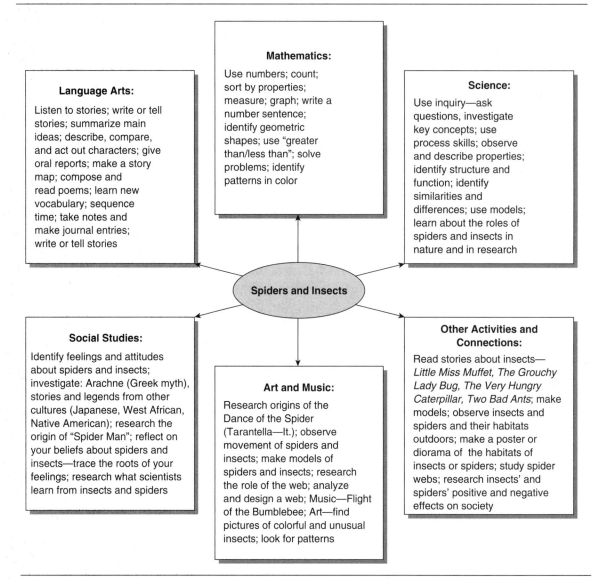

science; that is, they should be introduced and modeled by teachers and used by students to describe their actions.

Give me a fish, I eat for a day. Teach me how to fish, I eat for a lifetime.

Variation of a Chinese Proverb

Science Process Skills

Observation: the use of one or more of the senses to identify properties of objects and natural phenomena. Scientific investigation begins with making observations.

Classification: a system or method for arranging or distributing objects, events, or information. Classification systems range from simple to complex.

Making Inferences: tentative explanations for an observation; conclusions based on logic and reasoning; inferences are based on observations.

Prediction: forecasting future events or conditions; predictions allow us to use what we know and extend our thinking to what we do not know.

Measurement: making quantitative observations by comparing objects, events, or other phenomena to a conventional or nonconventional standard.

Using Numbers: counting and creating categories; applying mathematical rules or formulas.

Creating Models: using two- or three-dimensional graphic illustrations or other multisensory representations to communicate ideas or concepts.

Defining Operationally: naming or defining objects, events, or phenomena on the basis of their functions and/or identified characteristics.

Identifying Variables: recognizing factors or events that are held constant or likely to change under certain conditions during an experiment; the independent (manipulated) variable is one that is being tested to determine its effect on the dependent (responding) variable; controlled variables are those that are consistent throughout an experiment.

Formulating Hypotheses: making statements that are tentative and testable; a special type of prediction that suggests relationships between independent and dependent variables.

Recording and Interpreting Data: collecting, storing (through writing, drawing, audio or visual display, etc.), and analyzing information that has been obtained through the senses; making sense of data by determining patterns or relationships.

Drawing Conclusions: making summary statements that follow logically from data collected throughout an experience or experiences.

Dispositions

Dispositions define the character and/or work of the scientist (as well as other professionals), and they are valued by the profession and by society. Goals of science education based on "the learning of science through the doing of science" allow students to develop, practice, and model these dispositions throughout their lives.

Dispositions That Underlie Science

Curiosity and a Desire for Knowledge: an innate or developed desire for knowing and understanding the world.

Cooperation: a shared discussion of ideas, theories, and techniques at the local, state, national, and international levels.

Having Confidence in and Relying on Data: respect for evidence, which also implies the testing and retesting of ideas and monitoring of one's own thinking processes.

Comfort With Ambiguity: the results of science are always tentative; testing and retesting provide more confidence in one's conclusions; ambiguity gives rise to new problems and questions.

Respect for Living Things: all living things deserve human care both in the lab and in the field. Our attitudes toward the care and handling of live organisms say much about our value systems as human beings.

Willingness to Modify Explanations: additional data or reinterpretations of existing data may require us to modify explanations for phenomena and events; willingness to rethink conclusions is often one of science and science learning's most difficult personal decisions.

Respecting and Trusting the Thinking Process: science is an active process defined by patterns of reasoning that lead to theory building and theory testing; trust in the process is an essential element.

Intelligence and Dispositions

An interesting perspective on intelligence is offered by Ron Ritchart (2002). Dr. Ritchart believes that human intelligence lies not in ability, but rather in a set of dispositions or patterns of behavior. He identifies six dispositions that are central to intelligence.

These are:

- Curiosity
- Open-mindedness
- Reflective thought
- Strategic thought
- Skepticism
- A search for truth and understanding

By looking at cognitive ability as a set of behaviors that can be developed rather than as innate talent and intelligence then becomes something that can be taught. Intellectual character can transfer to other settings and can become an important part of K–12 education in general.

The dispositions that define intelligence are very similar to the dispositions that underlie science. These behaviors are valued and practiced by scientists and are addressed through high quality science instruction.

Thought and Discussion

Discuss ways to promote the development of process and thinking skills and the practice of dispositions in the classroom.

Revisit the Initial Question

How do standards clarify learning goals and inform the teaching/ learning process?

4

Creating a Context for Meaningful Learning

Indicators of High Quality Teaching

High Quality Teaching:

- Accommodates diversity through meaningful contexts
- Creates a context for meaningful learning

Building High Quality Materials to Inform High Quality Instruction

Step Four:

- Create a context for meaningful learning.

What are some important considerations for context that will make learning more meaningful for students?

AN INTRODUCTION TO CONTEXT

- Context equals the whole situation, background, or environment related to a particular event.
- The importance of context is linked to learning in a variety of ways by noted professionals.

Probably one of the most critical aspects of hemispheric specialization is the issue of context. Our understanding of what we read or our comprehension of what we hear depends on the context within which it occurs.

Pat Wolfe (2001)

Context gives language meaning. It enables the child to build on what he or she already knows to infer the meaning of new words and verbal constructs. For children who are learning science by means of an inquiry-centered approach, classroom investigations and the activities surrounding them can provide context . . . that can be springboards for growth in verbal fluency and literacy.

Douglas Lapp, National Science Resources Center (2001)

Learners in a positive, joyful environment are likely to experience enhanced learning, memory, and feelings of self-esteem.

Jensen (2000)

In this chapter, four perspectives of context are introduced, discussed, described in detail, and applied. The four perspectives are:

- Context as a function of interest and awareness of purpose
- Context and intellectual diversity
- Context embracing brain-based learning
- Context and cultural diversity

CONTEXT AS A FUNCTION OF INTEREST AND AWARENESS OF PURPOSE

In the classroom, students are engaged in activities ranging throughout the day from passive to active. The degree of meaning within a context is a function of many factors. One way to look at context is through two related factors: (1) the student's interest in the content and (2) the student's awareness of purpose of the instruction.

- The **interest** a student has in the subject is, in part, determined by the relevance of the content to the student's life and by the methods and strategies used to teach the subject matter.
- The student's **awareness of purpose** of the instruction is the degree to which the student perceives the content to be helpful or important in reaching educational or personal goals.

Figure 4.1 shows four possible relationships that exist between these two factors in the science classroom.

Figure 4.1   Interest and Awareness of Science in Relation to Student Learning

HIGH INTEREST/HIGH AWARENESS	HIGH INTEREST/LOW AWARENESS
Instruction	**Instruction**
• instruction is student-centered • students are aware of learning goals • instruction is part of a carefully crafted curriculum • teacher is facilitator • inquiry is primary method • concepts, skills, and dispositions are embedded in a high interest context that is challenging and relevant to the lives of students • thinking and problem solving are valued	• instruction not goal centered • teacher gives minimal attention to important goals • mediation of learning, thinking, and processing of information are minimal. • activities are engaging and fun • students are active
Student Response	**Student Response**
Science is interesting and challenging! Science is meaningful and it relates to my life. I like Science. I look forward to Science.	Science is fun! I like taking things apart. We play with a lot of cool stuff. Science is weird and mysterious. I don't understand science, but I like doing it.
LOW INTEREST/HIGH AWARENESS	LOW INTEREST/LOW AWARENESS
Instruction	**Instruction**
• little/no context • "test prep" and achievement focus • standards or benchmarks are driven with direct instruction • heavy emphasis on vocabulary and memorization of facts • reading, writing, and worksheet dependent	• little awareness of instructional goals • no context • text is curriculum • expository is the primary method • students read and answer questions • may read about current events or watch movies on relevant topics
Student Response	**Student Response**
I need to learn science for the test. This is important to the teacher. Science is a bunch of facts to memorize. Science has little relationship to my life. Everyone says science is important, but I don't know why.	Science is just stuff we read about. Science does not relate to me, so why do I have to learn this stuff? Science is boring! No more science for me!

Thought and Discussion

1. Give examples of when you have heard students respond in one or more of the ways described in the chart. Describe the conditions when the positive or negative responses occur.

2. Provide some practical suggestions for increasing interest and awareness in the science classroom.

CONTEXT AND INTELLECTUAL DIVERSITY

Messages from Learning Theory

Cognitive researchers, such as David Perkins, Mihaly Csikszentmihalyi, and Howard Gardner, long ago discovered that learners do not simply understand universally accepted knowledge in the same way. Rather, their theories support the notion that understanding and ways of knowing are personally developed through complex interactions of thinking processes, stored knowledge, and experiences.

Ways of knowing vary with gender, personal interest, and expertise in a subject area. For example, males process information differently than females; artists, scientists, writers, and other professionals express understanding in different ways. Because of the complexity of information processing and the unique ways learners create meaning, the effective instructional program must provide a variety of approaches and pathways to accommodate individual differences and maximize opportunities for learning.

Howard Gardner's (1999) Theory of Multiple Intelligences points to diversity in the ways that humans learn and know. He defines intelligence as "a biophysical potential to process information that can be activated in a cultural setting to solve problems or create products that are of value in a culture" (pp. 33–34).

Intelligences are perceived as potentials ready to be activated, and the ability of a potential to be realized is dependent on such things as the culture, nature of experiences, and motivation of the learner.

In our efforts to address diversity in the classroom, it is important to keep in mind that most students associate with more than one of the intelligences, and exposure to a variety of instructional strategies is more likely to increase learning potential among a group of students. Table 4.1 offers a list of Gardner's Eight Intelligences and identifies instructional strategies that may activate that intelligence. Strategies are tools to be used in the construction of meaningful contexts. They are creative approaches that are continuously redesigned and enhanced to meet the individual needs of learners.

Thought and Discussion

1. Consider Howard Gardner's (1999) quote:

   I would happily send my children to a school that takes differences among children seriously, that shares knowledge about differences with children and parents, that encourages children to take responsibility for their own learning, and that presents materials in such a way that each child has the maximum opportunity to master those materials and to show others and themselves what they have learned and understood. (pp. 91–92)

   What changes would be necessary in traditional schools to accommodate Gardner's vision?

2. What implications does the Theory of Multiple Intelligences have for curriculum development, classroom instruction, and assessment?

Table 4.1   Types of Intelligences and Sample Classroom Strategies That Activate Them

Intelligence	Strategies
Linguistic	• Reading/vocabulary development through discussion or games and puzzles • Formal speech; debate and impromptu speaking; humor and storytelling • Notebook-keeping; creative writing
Mathematical	• Use of abstract symbols; number sequences/pattern games • Use of graphic organizers • Use of metric and systems of measurement • Calculation and problem solving
Spatial	• Guided imagery and imagination • Mapping; technological design • Exploring patterns and designs • Making models; drawings and painting
Musical	• Music composition and creation • Investigate instrumental and natural sounds • Exploring vocal sounds and patterns • Humming and singing • Musical performances
Body-Kinesthetic	• Role-playing, drama, mime, and dance • Physical exercises; sports and games • Physical models and graphs
Interpersonal	• Cooperative/collaborative learning • Person-to-person communication • Peer review and interviews • Group projects
Intrapersonal	• Silent reflection • Focusing and concentration • Thinking strategies and reasoning • Metacognition
Naturalistic	• Observing and exploring natural phenomena • Questioning and investigating • Inventing and researching • Organizing and patterning thought • Designing action plans • Making models • Using the outdoors to learn and play

Activity: Analysis of a Case Study

1. Review the case study and identify in what ways interest and awareness of purpose and strategies for multiple intelligences are addressed through the role-playing activity.

2. Identify some of the learning goals that were addressed through the role-playing activity.

Case Study: Women in Science

Early in the school year, Ms. Wright, a fifth grade math and science teacher, noticed that the fourth grade end-of-grade math scores for her female students were significantly lower than those of the male students. As she got acquainted with her students, she realized that the female students lacked confidence not only in their ability to do math, but also in other aspects of learning as well.

Ms. Wright decided it was time to pay tribute to women as professionals and chose a theme of "Women in Science" for an all-class project. Her goals for the project were to introduce students to the many contributions women have made to the advancement of science throughout history, foster self-esteem in all students through the design and delivery of a public address, and expose students, both male and female, to careers in science.

All class members were given an assignment to select and research information about a woman who had made or is making a significant contribution to any field of science. Students selected scientists that were of interest to them and did research and wrote papers about the scientists and their contributions. Students shared their findings with others in the class. The history of science was relived in the fifth grade classroom.

The students were then invited to participate in the creation of a "wax museum" honoring the scientists, where they would portray (role-play) the scientist and give a short presentation to museum visitors about her major contributions. Students were not required to participate in the activity, nor was there any type of penalty for those who chose not to participate.

Students, both male and female, eagerly accepted the invitation to participate in the creation of the wax museum. In part, students were motivated by the opportunity to research and represent a famous scientist in an area of science of their choice, including aeronautics, medicine, and microbiology.

Students worked collaboratively to design costumes and gather props for each scientist they would portray. They wrote and practiced short speeches that they would give when visitors to the museum requested information about their scientists. The auditorium in the school was reserved for several days of rehearsals and performances. After several rehearsals, the wax museum was open to the public. Parents, teachers, entire classes of students, central office administrators and staff, and community members were invited to visit the wax museum.

The "wax figures," wearing their costumes and holding one or more props representing their scientists' areas of study, were stationed around the perimeter of the auditorium. They were posed in fixed, "waxlike" positions. Visitors were given directions to approach any figure and press a "button" that would activate the wax figure. The scientist would then "come alive," tell who she is or was, and describe what her major contribution is or was to the field of science. Some student scientists used their props as part of their explanations. After a short speech, the scientist resumed her original fixed position and awaited the next visitor. All students took their roles very seriously, and it was obvious that the students were enjoying their performances.

The visitors, as well as the students, learned of the many contributions of women scientists, such as physicist Marie Curie, primatologist Jane Goodall, biologist and geneticist Mary Styles Harris, theoretical physicist Shirley Ann Jackson, astronauts Sally Ride and Eileen Collins, and marine biologist Sylvia Earle. The wax museum project was a huge success!

SOURCE: Compliments of Heather Wright, Moore County, NC

CONTEXT EMBRACING BRAIN-BASED LEARNING

Much has been written describing relationships between brain functioning and the teaching/learning process. For example, we know that learning requires the development of neural networks within the brain and that learning involves not only our physical well-being, but also is a function of our emotions and attitudes. Educators, in particular, are interested in findings from brain research and are quick to make inferences related to classroom instruction. These inferences are often tested through action research in the classroom.

Rosenthal and Jacobsen report that the single greatest influence on learners is the classroom climate, since within a classroom of positive challenge and joy the body releases endorphins, molecules that elevate feelings and cause one to feel good (Jensen, 2000). Jensen (2000) supports this notion. "Learners in a positive, joyful environment are likely to experience enhanced learning, memory, and feelings of self-esteem" (p. 108).

Research tells us that one factor linked to learning is a state of relaxed alertness, which is required for the brain to make the maximum number of brain connections (Caine & Caine, 1991). "In a state of relaxed alertness, students are challenged within a context of safety. Their sense of purpose is readily invoked by an appropriate theme that serves to orient and focus their experience" (pp. 138–139).

Caine and Caine (1997) describe a state of being called downshifting that occurs when individuals perceive an experience as threatening. They describe downshifting as a psychophysiological response to threat associated with perceived helplessness. The condition affects high order cognitive functions in the brain and inhibits the brain's ability to actively process information.

Conditions that contribute to downshifting are:

1. Prespecified "correct" outcomes have been established by an external agent.

   Students must learn the answers the teacher has determined to be correct, and teachers must perform in ways that others deem correct.

2. Personal meaning is limited; what is to be learned or taught does not connect with what students know or desire to know.

3. Rewards and punishments are externally controlled and relatively immediate.

4. Work to be done is relatively unfamiliar, with little support available.

5. Isolation exacerbates uncertainty without the reassurance of immediate feedback. (Modified from Caine & Caine, 1997)

Underlying these conditions is a belief structure that denies the learner's purpose and meanings.

In order to counter downshifting, the educational environment must promote a state of mind that is optimal for meaningful learning. The Caine and Caine (1991) offer optimal conditions for meaningful learning:

- a relaxed nervous system,
- a sense of safety and mental, emotional, and physical security, and
- student self-motivation that is critical to the expansion of knowledge beyond the surface levels. (p. 131)

Robert Sylwester (2000) describes a similar condition called "learned helplessness" which results from a student living in an insecure, fearful environment. In this situation, a child senses no control and gives up the innate drive to cope. Further, he concludes that ". . . chronically fearful home and school environments can biologically diminish a student's ability to learn and remember" (p. 41).

Figure 4.2 shows a cause and effect relationship exists between levels of brain stimulation and learning.

Figure 4.2   Degree of Brain Stimulation and Response

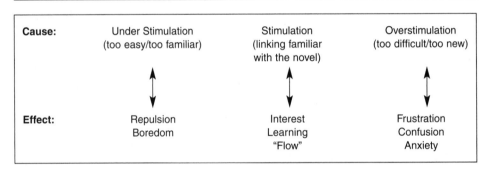

EMOTIONAL INTELLIGENCE AND LEARNING

One of the greatest joys of teaching is the experience of working with students who are totally engaged in an activity and express disappointment when they are interrupted or have to stop to change classes. When students are focused on a task in a relaxed, yet concentrated state, their brains are operating at peak efficiency. They are absorbed and enjoying the learning experience.

"Flow" is the term used by Mihaly Csikszentmihalyi, a University of Chicago psychologist, to describe a state of peak performance that represents "the ultimate in harnessing the emotions in the service of performance and learning." Flow represents a state of emotional intelligence where "the emotions are not just contained and channeled, but positive, energized and aligned with the task at hand" (Goleman, 1995, p. 90).

There are many barriers to reaching a state of flow in the classroom.

Figure 4.3   Barriers to Flow

Impulsive behavior, anxiety, worry, immediate gratification, lack of persistence, and fear of failure are just a few of the emotional states that interfere with attaining the relaxed alertness that is needed for maximum learning. Some ways teachers can reduce the emotional barriers that inhibit learning are to provide:

- clear learning goals linked to standards and lives of students
- a safe, risk-free, and supportive environment where students are allowed to learn through their mistakes, make choices, and vary their approaches to learning
- challenging activities that are interesting and meaningful
- guided practice of skills and strategies for learning
- a positive appreciation for persistence, delayed gratification, and other positive emotional behaviors
- frequent feedback about learning
- multiple opportunities for relearning and extended learning

Creating a meaningful context for learning maximizes the potential for students to enter a state of flow. "People seem to concentrate best when the demands on them are a bit greater than usual, and they are able to give more than usual. If there is too little demand on them, people are bored. If there is too much for them to handle, they get anxious. Flow occurs in that delicate zone between boredom and anxiety" (Csikszentmihalyi, in Goleman, 1995, pp. 91–92).

Implications for the Classroom

Classrooms need to provide experiences that increase the students' perceptions of their ability to control outcomes in order to develop confidence and restore or maintain the natural state of the brain to be motivated and curious.

Marian Diamond (Diamond & Hopson, 1998), noted brain researcher, describes an enriched environment for learning as one that is:

- free of stress and pressure
- provides positive emotional support
- ensures a nutritious diet
- provides social interactions
- presents opportunities for sensory stimulation through active participation in appropriately challenging activities

The enriched environment permits and even encourages "risk-taking," which is necessary for knowledge acquisition and the development of higher order thinking and problem solving to occur.

Thought and Discussion

1. Consider the interest/awareness of purpose chart, strategies related to the multiple intelligences, conditions related to downshifting, conditions of enriched environments, relationships between emotions and learning, and factors related to the degree of brain stimulation.

2. Discuss some implications of these messages for enriching the context, conditions, and approaches to instruction in the classroom and increasing the possibility that students will operate in a state of "flow."

CONTEXT AND CULTURAL DIVERSITY

The question of "what do we know about education and diversity, and how do we know it" was the focus of a four-year study funded by the Carnegie Corporation of New York www.newhorizons.org/strategies/multicultural/banks.htm (Banks et al., 2001) .

The findings of the Multicultural Consensus Panel were synthesized into a set of essential principles that describe ways in which educational policy and practice related to diversity can be improved. They support the notion that democratic societies depend on a thoughtful citizenry that believes in democratic ideals and is willing to participate in the civic life of the nation. Further, they contend that public schools are the key to maintaining a free and democratic society.

> The panel found that textbooks and teacher-designed lessons often present historical events, concepts, and issues from a single point of view (generally, the victor) and, often, do not help students understand how events and concepts relate to different groups of people who were involved in them.
>
> One of their recommendations: "Teaching students the different, and often conflicting, meanings of concepts and issues for the diverse groups that make up the U.S. population will help them to better understand the complex factors that contributed to the birth, growth, and development of the nation." (Banks et al., 2001, p. 198)

Dr. Gerry Madrazo (1998) supports the notion that a multicultural curriculum fosters respect for diversity. "A multicultural curriculum results in respect for diversity flowing from knowledge. With that respect will come the ability of people to live and work together in a diverse society" (p. 22).

SCIENCE IN MULTICULTURAL CONTEXTS

Consideration might be given to the ways that different cultures such as Native American, African American, Asian, Hispanic, and others, view the concepts or principles of science.

One approach is to compare and contrast cultural perspectives with contemporary views. For example, when studying the natural world, elementary students might consider such questions as:

- How did early Native Americans (or other cultures) explain the Sun and the heavenly bodies?
- What animals are considered "sacred" in some cultures and why?
- Why are some animals feared in some cultures?
- What plants were historically used as food or medicine by different cultures?
- What significance do certain minerals and/or gems have in different cultures?
- Why were early civilizations built with certain types of building materials?

Stories and legends offer a wonderful way to study history and to celebrate diversity in the classroom. Stories and legends often are handed down from generation to generation to explain events in nature. They give insights into the ways that early civilizations interpreted natural phenomena long before there were materials, mathematical formulas, and records to explain them. Early people made inferences and invented stories to explain the wonders they observed.

A Standards-Based Science Unit in a Multicultural Context

The unit described here provides a model for how the eight steps for the development of high quality instructional materials can be applied to a theme in a cultural context.

***Steps One–Three: Topic/Theme*—**Interdependence of Plants and Animals

Standards and key concepts and processes: Standards-based concepts may be addressed through the study of an ecosystem or variety of ecosystems including those related to:

- the roles of light, range of temperatures, and soil composition in an ecosystem's capacity to support life
- the structure and functions of organisms within the population of an ecosystem: producers, consumers, decomposers; the variety and numbers of organisms an ecosystem can support
- the Sun as the source of energy for an ecosystem; the flow of energy and interactions of organisms within a system (food chain/food web)

In addition, students will use process skills of science to investigate concepts and solve problems and to develop thinking skills and practice valued dispositions.

Step Four: Create a Context

When designing the context for instruction, it is important to consider the ways that learning in a cultural context will make standards-based concepts more relevant to the lives of the students in your classroom. In a multicultural classroom, students may explore the same questions related to their own culture, or they may divide into groups with each group investigating a different culture and sharing their findings. In any event, the key concepts from state or local standards remain the same. What is different are the ways that students investigate and learn the concepts and principles. Throughout the unit, students should research the cultural significance of the concepts they are studying.

Figure 4.4   A Multicultural Approach to Learning

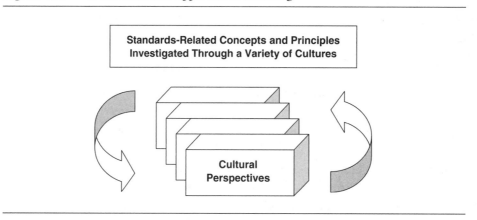

Investigating the Key Concepts and Principles of Elementary Science Through Native American Culture

Sample Inquiry Questions

1. What were the connections of diverse groups of people (in this case, Native Americans) to the ecosystems in which they lived?

2. In what ways did people depend on the Earth? What were their beliefs and attitudes about plants and animals, the Earth and sky, and natural phenomena?

3. How were the living and nonliving components of the Earth represented in songs and stories?

4. What do those songs and stories tell us about the relationships between people and the Earth?

5. How did beliefs and attitudes of the Native Americans about natural phenomena compare to the beliefs and attitudes of other cultures or the culture in which you now live?

Figure 4.5 shows a K-W-L Chart that might be used to determine what students know and would like to know about the research questions.

Figure 4.5   K-W-L Chart

What I Know	What I Would Like to Know	What I Learned

Step Five: Consider Learning Activities and Experiences

Reading #1: Susan Jeffers (1991), *Brother Eagle, Sister Sky: A Message from Chief Seattle*

Summary: "This we know: All things are connected like the blood that unites us. We did not weave the web of life, we are merely a strand in it. Whatever we do to the web, we do to ourselves" (words of Chief Seattle).

Reading #2: "How Grandmother Spider Stole the Sun" in Michael J. Caduto and Joseph Bruchac (1989), *Keepers of the Earth: Native American Stories and Environmental Activities for Children.*

Summary: The animals wanted light; the bear heard there was something called the Sun on the other side of the world. The fox burned his mouth trying to take a piece and the possum burned off her tail trying to hide a piece of the Sun. Grandmother spider wove a bag out of her webbing and put a piece of the Sun into it. She was able to successfully bring it to the dark side of the Earth. The buzzard was chosen to put the Sun up high so all could see and benefit from it because he could fly the highest. Buzzard makes a great sacrifice when he brings the Sun to the highest point in the sky for all to see. The feathers on his head burn off and his skin becomes red. He is honored for his gift of giving. "And because Grandmother Spider brought the Sun in her bag of webbing, at times the sun makes rays across the sky which are shaped like the rays in Grandmother Spider's web. It reminds everyone that we are all connected, like the strands of Grandmother Spider's web, and it reminds everyone of what Grandmother Spider did for all the animals and the people" (p. 50).

Key Concepts Addressed in the Story

- The Sun's energy is important for supporting life on Earth.
- There is a flow of energy among plants and animals; the process of photosynthesis in green plants requires energy from the Sun.
- Photosynthesis produces food in green plants upon which animals are dependent and is the basis for food chains and food webs.
- Day and night, a continuous cycle, occur because the Earth rotates on its axis once every 24 hours.

A descriptive map showing the relationships between concepts is shown in Figure 4.6.

Reading Comprehension: Discuss the meaning of the stories, including the ethics, values, and beliefs. Have students select information related to key concepts and write a summary of each story in their notebooks. They should identify new vocabulary words, new facts and information, and new questions to investigate.

Standards-Based Activities for Basic Learning, Relearning, or Extended Learning: A variety of hands-on/investigative activities related to standards-based concepts and instructional goals can be developed. Some ideas are:

- Use the school grounds or local park to explore your ecosystem; identify plants and animals that inhabit your local ecosystem and identify some of the adaptations these organisms have developed to survive in the ecosystem.
- Compare the features of the local ecosystem with features of ecosystems inhabited by early Native American cultures.

Figure 4.6 Relationships Between Concepts for Interdependence of Plants and Animals

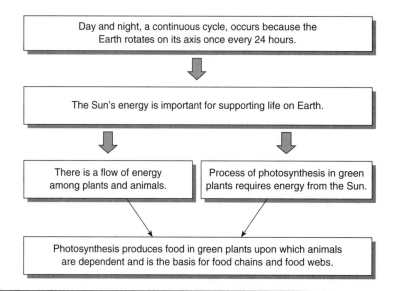

- Investigate the Sun as a source of energy for food chains/food webs.
- Investigate photosynthesis and describe its importance in the transfer of energy in an ecosystem; identify the Sun's role in photosynthesis.
- Investigate interactions of organisms in an ecosystem; classify the organisms by their role: producer, consumer, or decomposer.
- Grow a variety of plants to determine the role of light, temperature, soil, water, and space in supporting life.
- Identify problems and issues related to "unbalanced" populations within ecosystems.
- Research to discover natural artifacts that have significance to the culture you are studying; identify what parts of living or nonliving things these artifacts represent.
- Make posters or models of ecosystems, food chains/food webs, or artifacts.

Strategies for Differentiated Learning: Use an array of strategies throughout the instructional process and provide opportunities for students to relearn concepts or to extend learning, as needed. Centers may be set up in various parts of the classroom and be used to:

- display artifacts, such as collections of shells, fossils, specimens, and so forth, or models
- provide references for extended reading or research
- provide a place to create models of artifacts or work on projects
- provide a quiet place to read or write stories, poems, or plays incorporating concepts or artifacts
- display student-made visuals such as posters, brochures, graphic organizers, and models
- provide the materials and directions for independent or small group activities for relearning or extended learning
- provide computers for Internet research

Students may engage in role-play or simulations as part of their study. Reenactments of significant events, dance, cultural sports and games, and other forms of creative expression may enhance the learning experience for some students.

Other students may design projects or develop action plans for investigating an area of interest. Independent research through resources or the Internet may answer questions that arise throughout investigations and discussions. Surveys or interviews with family members, professionals, and community members can be used to gather information and opinions.

What is important to remember throughout the design of instruction is that activities should be linked in some meaningful way to the standards-based concepts and instructional goals around which the unit is developed. There is not one way to learn or to know important concepts. It is important to allow students to explore concepts in a variety of ways and to demonstrate their learning in a variety of ways.

Step Six: Framing Thought and Making Connections

Using Questions: Questions focusing on the processes of learning and the key concepts are important for each activity and experience. Questions related to the cultural context should be designed to allow students to make comparisons between "ways of knowing" in a historical context and "ways of knowing" in the contemporary context or to compare ways of knowing between two contemporary cultural contexts. The application of the concepts to social/cultural contexts provides opportunities for students to engage in higher order thinking and develop an understanding of other cultures.

Sample Questions Related to the Cultural Context—Native Americans

1. What were the connections of diverse groups of people to the ecosystems in which they lived?

2. In what ways did the people depend on the Earth? What were their beliefs and attitudes about plants and animals, the Earth and sky, and natural phenomena?

3. What do their artifacts tell us about their beliefs or their values?

4. How were the living and nonliving components of the Earth represented in songs and stories?

5. What do those songs and stories tell us about the relationships between people and the Earth?

6. How do the beliefs and attitudes of the Native Americans about natural phenomena compare to the beliefs and attitudes of other cultures about natural phenomena or to those of the culture in which you now live?

Using Notebooks: Notebook entries will be determined by the actual activities that are selected to address the key concepts and skills. Some entries might be:

- completed K-W-L chart with a summary of learning
- descriptions of investigations and activities
- data tables, charts, and graphs; drawings; conclusions; reflections; new questions
- answers to questions showing evidence of concept understanding
- summary of ways that the Native Americans interpreted and explained natural phenomena
- action plans for projects and research; results of research
- illustrations of models
- samples of writing, poems, stories, and so forth

Step Seven: Design a Rich Assortment of Assessments

Determine ways to gather evidence of student learning throughout the instructional process. Revisit the standards and important concepts and skills identified in Steps One–Three and consider ways to gather evidence of student learning throughout the instructional phase.

For example, some possible embedded assessments are:

- checklists showing student participation in discussion and activities
- records of the quality of work done by the student during investigations and research
- completed data tables and lab reports
- notebook entries and reflections for each activity
- products such as models, charts, graphs, posters, illustrations, poems, and before stories
- evidence of concept understanding in verbal, visual, and written work
- K-W-L chart and other visuals accurate and completed
- written comparisons of cultural perspectives
- summaries of research, interviews, projects, and other extended learning
- open response quizzes

Step Eight: Materials and Equipment and Other Considerations for Instruction

An equipment and materials list should be developed based on the activities and experiences that are included in the instructional unit. Be sure that safety is addressed in each activity and experience.

Instruction may be differentiated through the use of centers, tiered instruction, and projects. Some of the other ways to structure learning to meet the needs of all students are described in Chapter 5.

Thought and Discussion

Analysis of Model Unit

1. In what ways did the sample unit address standards and instructional goals?

2. In what ways did the sample unit address cultural diversity?

3. How would the unit of instruction be different if the majority of students were African American? Hispanic? Asian? Other?

4. What are some other ways to address cultural diversity in units of instruction?

Revisit the Initial Question

What are some important considerations for context that will make learning more meaningful for students?

Methods, Strategies, and Best Practices for High Quality Instruction

Indicators of High Quality Teaching

High Quality Teaching:

- Includes varied methods that engage and challenge students intellectually and address prior learning, misconceptions, and new learning
- Embeds strategies that allow students to develop new or modified thinking frames with links to their own lives, technology, and issues relevant to their community, state, nation, and world

Building High Quality Materials to Inform High Quality Instruction

Step Five:

- Research learning activities and experiences. Consider those that are readily available.
- Determine activities to be developed or modified.
  - Use a consistent format for crafting each instructional activity and experience.
  - Include multiple and varied methods and strategies for meeting the needs of learners.
  - Consider activities and experiences for relearning and for extended learning.

What methods, strategies, and best practices will enhance the quality of the curriculum and strengthen the instructional process?

THE ROLE OF METHODS IN UNIT DEVELOPMENT

The activities and experiences that are selected for the instructional program should be linked to important learning goals and standards. A distinction should be made between activities that reinforce what students already know and those that add to learning, since there are many activities that rely on information that students already know and do not take them to new levels of learning.

Finding out what students know about a topic is important for uncovering misconceptions and for establishing a baseline of knowledge on which to build. Worthwhile learning activities and experiences are those that add to the students' knowledge base, develop skills ability, or strengthen valued dispositions in some meaningful way.

National and state standards documents point to inquiry as the strategy used by scientists to uncover the mysteries of the universe. Traditionally, science education has identified five basic methods for teaching. These methods are:

- **Expository**—lectures, media presentations, guest speakers, text material, pictures, CD-ROMs, audiotapes and videotapes, trade books, and the like
- **Discussion**—student to student or teacher to student exchange of ideas and information
- **Demonstrations by the teacher without student input**
- **Demonstrations with teacher-student interactions**
- **Guided Inquiry**—student- or teacher-generated questions and activities with varying degrees of structure, leading to a range of predictable outcomes or expectations
- **Open Inquiry/Problem-Based Learning**—student- or teacher-generated inquiry questions and activities without focused and/or predicted outcomes or expectations

Expository: A lecture is an abstract form of communication that transfers information from person to person. Learners either remember what they hear as words or attempt to create meaning by forming mental images. In the science classroom, expository teaching takes the form of telling facts, information, or a story; writing information on a board or transparency for students to copy; showing a film or videotape; or reading text.

Discussion: Discussion is effective when students have had experiences that reach beyond an awareness level and/or bring a wealth of prior knowledge or generated data to the table. Good discussion takes place in a nonthreatening environment where students' ideas and opinions are respected and where they will not be rewarded or punished for their understanding or misunderstanding.

In an inquiry classroom, discussion questions might focus on designs of investigations, processes that were used, data that were collected, and/or conclusions that were drawn relative to investigations or research. Discussions centered on discrepant events or data may lead to problem solving and the generation of new inquiry questions. Discussions may lead to conflict resolution or debate of an issue. The applications of science to technology and/or society (especially environmental issues) provide an arena for worthwhile discussion.

Demonstration: Demonstrations involve one or more persons giving a presentation to an audience that may vary in size from a small group to an entire class. Generally, the audience is expected to observe and discover phenomena. Demonstrations may be valuable or necessary when:

- The materials and/or equipment involved are costly and/or delicate.
- The equipment, materials, or process is not safe for students to use themselves.
- A visitor is showing/describing work or a small set of samples that are fragile or valuable.
- There is a person or animal involved.
- Safety is an issue.
- There is only one opportunity for an event to happen.

Students should be responsible for doing something during a demonstration, such as recording observations, answering questions, completing a chart, or collecting data. Demonstrations with interactions allow students to have input and to ask questions. The exchange of dialog between teacher and student(s) can be enlightening and informative for all students.

There are a few problems associated with demonstrations. Sometimes students do not understand what they should be observing and are not given opportunities to ask questions. Some students may be unable to view the demonstration well because of distance or position.

Guided Inquiry: Traditionally, "guided discovery" was the name given to hands-on activities and laboratory investigations that led the learner to a predetermined or a predictable data set or response. This approach was used to verify knowledge following a lecture or reading from a text.

Inquiry is defined in national standards as an active, hands-on/minds-on approach to learning. Inquiry involves posing questions (teacher- or student-generated) and developing action plans for answering them. Through inquiry, students:

- design action plans for investigating the questions
- make predictions (hypotheses)
- engage in activities using a variety of materials and equipment

Inquiry involves the use of process and thinking skills, use of tools and technologies to gather data, analysis and interpretation of data, and posing plausible solutions or conclusions. Generally, in inquiry activities, there is a range of data that support or do not support the predictions. The quality of the data is a function of the quality of the procedures. Students come to recognize the importance of data as evidence to support conclusions.

Figure 5.1 shows the range of structure for inquiry-based activities from most structured activities with predictable outcomes to least structured problem-based inquiries.

Figure 5.1   Range of Structure for Inquiry-Based Activities

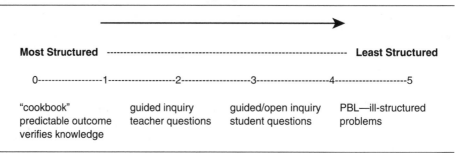

Open Inquiry/Problem-Based Learning: Open inquiry implies a less formal structure for dealing with student-generated questions and may be based on such things as:

- observations
- activities or experiences
- real-world problems
- ill-structured problems
- defense of a position

Problem-based learning (PBL) is a strategy based on focused, experiential learning that is organized around the investigation and resolution of messy, real-world problems. Problem-based learning is both a curriculum organizer and an instructional strategy. Torp and Sage (1998) identify three main characteristics of problem-based learning:

- Engages students as stakeholders in a problem situation
- Organizes curriculum around a holistic problem, enabling students to learn in relevant and connected ways
- Creates a learning environment in which teachers coach student thinking and guide student inquiry, facilitating deeper levels of understanding. (p. 14)

Problem-based learning strategies were used in middle school field research projects with results reported by Musial and Hammerman (1997). They describe the perspective of PBL learners in this way:

The problem-based learner tends to develop mental patterns that are highly connected to the richness of the problem situation. Such understanding is highly integrated and linked to a variety of real-world situations, perspectives, and disciplines. In answering essay questions, learners are able to elaborate on the meaning of important ideas and add nuances that are connected to the real world. This is so, not because they have read about those connections, but because they have experienced the connections firsthand. (p. 6)

TEACHER'S ROLE IN INQUIRY

With high quality materials at hand, teachers are free to be the facilitators of learning. When teachers assume the role of facilitators, students become stakeholders in the learning process and are more likely to take ownership for their learning,

As facilitators, teachers can interact with students in small groups or individually to affirm or correct their work, listen to their ideas and explanations, and make sure they are not misinterpreting or misunderstanding processes or data. In this climate, teachers can ask higher level questions, share their thinking with students, and guide them toward successful strategies.

Following investigations, teacher- or student-led discussions should focus on student experience, data, and conclusions related to the inquiry question. Students should not be left on their own to make interpretations of data and experiences, since misconceptions may arise. By asking thoughtful questions, teachers help students reflect on their experiences; make sense of data; connect learning to prior knowledge; create meaning; apply learning to their lives, technology, and society; and determine the next steps for extended learning.

DIRECT INSTRUCTION VERSUS INQUIRY-BASED INSTRUCTION

Investigations and experiences that guide the learner to understand key concepts, develop skills, and practice valued dispositions should be selected with thought and care. Table 5.1 describes some differences between direct instruction and inquiry-based teaching.

For example, in a traditional classroom, the concept "all organisms are made of cells, the fundamental unit of life" would be read and memorized. Pictures might supplement the text.

In an inquiry classroom, students would:

- use a microscope to make firsthand observations of various types of cells alone and in various types of tissues
- identify and describe the components common to cells and research their functions
- identify similarities and differences between plant and animal cells
- make models of cells showing the unique features of the organelles
- identify the unique structures and features of single-cell organisms
- use a graphic organizer or concept map to show the relationships between concepts
- explain, describe, show, or demonstrate what they learned in a variety of ways

Students can begin to assess their own knowledge and skills with the help of rubrics that focus on the attainment of standards-based concepts and skills. As students become familiar with the expectations for what they should know and be able to do, they are more likely to work toward those expected goals.

Table 5.1   Direct Instruction Versus Inquiry-Based Instruction

Direct Instruction	Inquiry-Based Instruction
Teach Is Tell Teacher presents information, and students verify through activity. Present concept: Today we are going to learn about X; X is . . . Now, we'll verify what I told you.	**Teach Is Wonder, Investigate, and Discover** Teacher or students present questions; students wonder and think What do you think we find when we . . . ? What will happen if . . . ? What is the relationship between . . . ? What will you do to find the answers to your questions?
Passive Learning Students read, write, research using resources and the Internet, watch videotapes, listen to others tell what they know, watch demonstrations, and so forth. Teachers function as providers of information.	**Active Learning** Students engage in a variety of activities that generate data or provide information; they ask questions, conduct investigations, do projects, and conduct action research; they apply learning to their lives, technology, and society; teachers function as facilitators.
Questioning Students generate questions, and questions are answered by teachers or found in references.	**Questioning** Students generate questions, and questions are investigated through activities, experiments, or experiences.
Reading/Discussion Students read current event articles from a science newspaper, magazine, or textbook and answer questions; students share answers to questions.	**Reading/Discussion** Students read and relate information to inquiry questions or related problems and issues; discussion includes reflections on process, presentations of perspectives, sharing of data, critical analyses, debates, and elaborations of learning.
Writing/Recording Students copy notes from a transparency while teacher lectures, take notes from a videotape or demonstration, and fill in formatted lab reports.	**Writing/Recording** Students use notebooks to record questions, make predictions, describe plans and strategies for investigating, create data tables and record data, write conclusions and supportive research, summarize learning, record applications, and draw graphic organizers, illustrations, and models.

Thought and Discussion

1. Consider the work of scientists. Inquiring scientists utilize all of the instructional methods as they investigate and solve problems.

2. Select a science topic that is familiar to you. Identify ways that each of the methods may be used to enhance learning of the concepts and skills related to that topic.

HIGH QUALITY LESSON PLANNING

An abundance of activities, investigations, and experiences exist for many science topics. It is not necessary to "reinvent the wheel" for ideas, but in many cases, it may be necessary to modify existing materials to address state-specific standards and to include important components of high quality.

Well-designed and developed activities contain elements of effective inquiry and best practices for student achievement. With thoughtful and consistent design, instructional activities can address standards and include methods, strategies, and best practices that are best suited to the needs and interests of learners.

Thoughtful Planning Guides Effective Teaching

An extended version of the Five E's Lesson Plan Format provides a framework for developing and delivering high quality lessons. Although there is some flexibility in the sequence of the steps, it is important to include all components of the plan. Here the headings for the "front matter"—title, overview, standards and concepts, instructional objectives, background information, and materials and safety concerns—are shown prior to the five E's.

MODIFIED FIVE E's LESSON PLAN FORMAT

Title of Activity:

A Brief Overview

Standards and Concepts

Select those standards that will be addressed in the lesson. After careful consideration of the meaning of the standard and the background information, select the key concept(s) that the activity or experience will address.

Instructional Objectives

Establish clear links to standards and benchmarks. Objectives guide and inform the direction of the investigation. Describe what students will know (key concepts) and be able to do (skills) as a result of this activity or experience.

Background Information

Provide a detailed explanation of the concepts that will be addressed in the lesson and provide additional information that would be helpful to know and resources to address questions and extensions.

Materials and Safety Concerns

List materials, equipment, and resources that will be needed for each group of students and for the teacher. You may specify a desirable number of students per group and other classroom arrangements, needs, and so forth that will add to the success of the lesson. Identify resources for extended learning and for relearning. Be sure to address all safety issues and concerns that pertain to the lesson.

The Five E's:

- **Engagement (Activating and Engaging; Identifying Misconceptions)**

Consideration should be given to creating a meaningful context to motivate students to investigate and apply skills and concepts. A K-W-L chart might be used to determine what students know and would like to know about a topic.

Some ways to enhance interest and promote "wonder" are:

1. Ask students what they know and would like to know about a topic, concept, or issue. This approach will help to identify misconceptions students have and allow them to ask questions around which further investigation and research can be structured.

2. Give students something to investigate and wonder about—an activity, experience, event, field trip.

3. Read an article about a science-related issue pertinent to the lives of students or to their community and find out what students know and would like to know about it.

4. Use a discrepant event to raise questions.

5. Read a letter, memo, or invitation from someone of importance to elicit student help with a project or an experiment.

6. Ask students to design an action plan for gathering information about an important topic.

- **Exploration (Discovery Phase)**

Identify an inquiry question or allow students to identify inquiry questions. What will students actually do?

In this phase, the teacher facilitates and guides the instructional process. It is important to describe procedures for guided inquiry clearly and accurately or establish a set of guidelines for student-constructed inquiries.

Process skill words should be used throughout, such as "the student will observe, make inferences, classify," and so forth.

Students should have to record data in words, numbers, or pictures and/or describe relationships, feelings, and questions.

If the activity is a guided inquiry, provide action plans for students to follow and data tables or challenge students to design action plans and data tables, if possible. Notebook entries should be made throughout the exploration phase.

- **Explanation (Processing for Meaning)**

Design a set of thought-provoking questions that allow students to explain what they did and reflect on what they learned.

Ask questions that allow students to share their ideas and build on prior knowledge and develop expanded frames of thought. Use student-generated data to support new learning. Create meaning through reflection and discussion.

Graphic organizers will enable students to visually show their understanding of concepts and relationships between concepts. Misconceptions may emerge as students describe and explain their understandings. Use good questioning strategies including "wait time" and show respect for student comments and questions.

- **Elaboration and Extension (Making Connections)**

Lessons become meaningful to students when applications are made to their lives and interests. Connections and applications should be made to technology and to society, including personal, family, community, state, national, and global issues.

Include opportunities for students to learn more or make needed clarifications (possibly based on misconceptions or new questions that arise) through further investigation or reading and Internet research.

Allow opportunities for relearning for students who do not show evidence of understanding.

- **Evaluation (Shaping Understanding)**

Use formative assessment strategies throughout the learning experience, such as notebook entries, data, informal questioning, and drawings and illustrations. Use graphics, reports, projects, presentations, teacher-made tests, and other assessment strategies that enable students to show and explain learning.

Examine ways to determine how new knowledge has expanded or changed the student's original understanding, "frame," or mental construct.

Evaluation may come before or after Elaboration and Extension. Elaboration and Extension may be important to the lesson as a whole and come before the Evaluation phase or may be optional and come after. Students who show successful completion of activities and understanding of concepts may extend learning through reading, writing, projects, products, or research. In some activities, Elaboration and Extension might be considered as separate phases. The order of these latter phases is not as important as their purpose and clarity.

(Modified from Rodger W. Bybee [2002] *Learning Science and the Science of Learning*, NSTA Press or reprinted from E. Hammerman [2005] *Eight Essentials of Inquiry-Based Science*, Corwin Press.)

STRATEGIES FOR STUDENT ENGAGEMENT

Strategies are approaches, activities, tasks, or conditions used in the instructional process. They are the creative ways to enhance basic methods and engage students. Strategies may be thought of as paint on an artist's palette. As teachers create their instructional plans, strategies add interest and excitement. Some ways strategies can be used are:

- as management tools, such as cooperative learning strategies
- as energizers and motivators, such as movement, humor, and instructional games
- for thinking and sharing ideas, such as "think-pair-share" or peer review
- to vary the instructional approach
- to differentiate instruction and offer choices
- for relearning and extended learning

A set of strategies for student-centered instruction are clustered under four headings in Table 5.2. The strategies are not exclusive to the headings, since most strategies are useful for a variety of purposes. It is important to be familiar with a wide range of strategies in order to build them into the instructional process.

Thought and Discussion

1. Give an example where you have used one or more of the instructional strategies (or seen one or more of them used) to enhance learning.

2. What other successful strategies that you know of might be added to the list? What other categories might be added?

STRATEGIES TO ENHANCE INQUIRY

Table 5.3 shows another way to cluster strategies using the Five E's model. The Lesson Planning Guide links a set of strategies that can be used to enhance the teaching/learning process to the various stages of inquiry.

In this guide, the Five E's Lesson Plan format is expanded to include seven stages. These stages are:

1. **Engagement I:** Provides purpose and motivation

2. **Engagement II:** Introduces inquiry questions; identifies context; clarifies expectations

3. **Exploration:** Process of instruction; what students will do

4. **Explanation I:** Reflecting on process and processing of data; student explanations

Table 5.2   Categories and Strategies for Effective Instruction

Management Tools	Energizers and Motivators	Thinking and Sharing	Enrichment
Learning Centers	Field trips	Think-Pair-Share	Give a demonstration; apply learning
Cooperative Groups	Essential questions	K-W-L Charts	Create songs, raps, poems, stories, dances
Teaming	Hands-on activities	Debate; role-play	Use the Internet
Jigsaw	Investigations	Use notebooks and graphics	Build models; make posters and visuals
Gallery Walk	Create action plans	Roundtable or panel discussion	Apply learning and technological design
Tiered Learning	Conduct interviews and surveys	Ask and explore new questions	Design and play instructional games
Stations	Guest speakers	Data analysis and graphing	Videotape, film, or broadcast
Contracts	Brainstorm ideas	Presentations	Design new products or projects
Individualized Instruction	Use outdoors	Process experiences; make connections	Explore careers in science and technology
Projects	Discrepant event	Peer review; reflective thought; self-assess	Illustrate and role-play a story

5. **Explanation II With Elaboration:** Framing thought and checking for understanding; making applications to technology and society

6. **Evaluation:** Evidence that learning has occurred

7. **Elaboration and Extension:** Conducting research; asking new questions; relating learning to situations and conditions beyond the classroom

Table 5.3   Lesson Planning Guide

Stages of Inquiry	Instructional Strategies	Application
1. Engagement I (Motivation and Purpose)	• Think, pair, share; brainstorm ideas • Dilemma or issue • K-W-L (What I know; What I want to know; What I learned) • Field trip • Role-play; simulation • Letter, announcement, appeal • Analysis of research • Discrepant event	
2. Engagement II (Inquiry Questions, Context, and Expectations)	• Use graphic organizers • Identify essential questions • Role-play; stories; simulations to define context • Ask questions related to a field experience • Ask questions related to natural phenomena; world problems or issues • Design action plans for learning	
3. Exploration (Process of Instruction)	• Inquiry-based activities • Field experiences • Use of notebooks • Observations and data collecting • Write, draw, or illustrate • Create visuals and models • Videotapes, software programs, Internet research • Cooperative learning; grouping; teaming • Jigsaw • Centers for enrichment or relearning • Stations • Guest speaker • Socratic dialogue • Instructional games • Role-play • Conduct interviews	
4. Explanation I (Processing Information)	• Analyze and graph data • Create and use visuals • Prepare and give presentations • Write a report • Discuss and compare results • Explain or describe findings • Connect learning to prior knowledge • Describe relationships	

Stages of Inquiry	Instructional Strategies	Application
5. **Explanation II with Elaboration (Framing Thought and Checking Understanding)**	• Create graphic organizers • Make connections to self, subject areas, careers, technology, and societal issues • Explain models • Defend a position • Describe meaning in new context • Give examples and recommendations	
6. **Evaluation**	• Notebook entries • Presentations • Products; projects • Models and visuals • Written reports and essays • Analyses of research • Self-assessments using rubrics • Peer reviews; interviews • Teacher-made tests	
7. **Elaboration and Extension (Applications, Research, and New Questions)**	• Apply concepts to self, technology, and society; create action plans for dealing with environmental problems and issues • Ask new questions • Create plans for independent study • Invent or design something new • Engage in Internet or action research • Perform community service	

CREATIVE ENGAGEMENT, INVOLVEMENT, AND ASSESSMENT

Special attention should be given to strategies to capture student attention, create interest, and motivate them. Units of instruction can be designed around creative approaches such as:

- An invitation from a scientist, school administrator, or other professional to assist with a research project
- An ad from a "help wanted" column from a celebrity
- A mysterious event or crime that needs to be solved
- Preparation for an excursion or field trip; preparation for a trip to Mars or other planet
- Making of a movie, play, or Power Point presentation; creation of an illustrated book that students can use to teach younger students about a concept; creation of a brochure that conveys a message

- A real-world problem or issue; a local environmental concern; a search for alternative solutions
- A study of physics during a visit to an amusement park

Students enjoy tackling problems, role-playing, and having fun while learning. These and other creative approaches spark student interest and motivate them to become involved in the learning process. Five examples of creative engagement and assessment are presented here; note the strategies that are used in each example.

EXAMPLE 1: Using Novelty to Engage Students

Strategies: Role-play; answering an ad; creating action plans

Tour With the Band

Help Wanted: Concert Manager for _____

After the successful release of their new CD, _____ is going on tour and needs a concert manager. Job responsibilities include managing the setup at the performance location, overseeing working condition of instruments, overseeing the sound and acoustic conditions in the concert halls, and taking care of accommodations for the band members.

The following qualifications are required. The applicant must:

1. Demonstrate an understanding of how sound is produced and how it travels, qualities of pitch and intensity, how different materials affect sound, and how instruments work.

2. Possess good communication skills—reading, writing, speaking, and listening—and be able to work effectively with others in a team.

3. Send a letter describing an action plan for learning and your qualifications following your learning experiences for this position.

EXAMPLE 2: Using New Environments for Exploration and Discovery

Strategies: Field experience to natural habitats; role-play; making maps; observation; data collecting; sharing of information; make applications to new situations

As an introduction to a unit on energy transfer in a living system, students will assume the role of a naturalist and explore the school grounds or nearby park to discover a variety of habitats for local animals. They will:

- make careful observations; map the locations of habitats
- describe the habitats for birds, insects, squirrels, and other animals in detail
- look for evidence of food at or near the habitat (i.e., observe animals feeding, nut shells near a habitat, or stored food near a site)
- infer the diet of local animals
- use their data and data collected by other groups to create food chains

Following a series of activities where students will learn about categories of organisms, trophic levels, and food chains/food webs, students will apply their learning to new environments.

Table 5.4   Science in Informal Settings

Informal Environments	Suggested Activities
Zoo, aquarium, aviary	• Investigate animal habitats. • Discover food chains for animals. • Observe exhibits and performances to determine characteristics of animals and their abilities to "perform."
Amusement park	• Investigate forces and motion in roller coasters and other rides. • Observe and investigate gravitational potential energy and kinetic energy.
Museum	• Observe specimens and models. • Learn about artifacts that relate to science content. • Interact with specimens, such as rocks and minerals, animal skulls, pelts, fossils, plants, and others. • Identify the characteristics of natural materials and artifacts.
Technology centers	• Observe the role of technology for enhancing data collection and measurement and use in visual displays. • Observe technological design. • Study relationships between structure and function in technology. • Use the tools of technology to solve problems and extend learning. • Identify strengths and limitations to technology. • Identify "trade-offs" in the use of technology for solving problems.
Parks, outdoor education centers, nature centers, botanic gardens, and other informal science centers	• Follow self-guided trails that lead to native specimens and natural phenomena. • Observe variety of plants and animals to identify unique features of organisms. • Attend performances and videotape presentations. • Engage in firsthand observation and activities, such as hunting for fossils, observing or collecting rocks, investigating cemeteries, planting trees, collecting sap to make maple syrup, and conducting investigations in fields and forests, ponds, lakes, or rivers.

Table 5.5   Novelty in Performance Assessment

Topic	Strategies	Activity	Assessment
Space Exploration	Role-playing; simulation; explanation	Design a spacecraft and a space station and simulate the trip to outer space. Students assume the role of the astronauts en route to outer space.	Students will describe concepts and explain how they applied the concepts from the unit of study to a new situation.
Forensic Science	Role-playing; apply learning; apply and describe techniques; collect and record data; use logic and reasoning; draw conclusions	Students will examine a "crime scene." They will conduct investigations, make observations and inferences, and apply tests. They will collect and examine fingerprints and use chromatography to gather evidence.	Students will explain their procedures and findings. They will use data to explain their inferences and conclusions about the guilt or innocence of suspects.

EXAMPLE 3: Using Informal Science Centers to Enrich Learning

Strategies: Field trip; outdoor education; firsthand experience

Students can assume any number of roles and responsibilities when visiting informal science centers. Out of school experiences are exciting for students, especially if they have not had these types of experiences previously. The excitement of the experience can be enhanced with a focus on discovery and learning. A well-planned and organized experience can be very educationally rewarding.

EXAMPLE 4: Using Performance Assessments

Performance assessments engage students in worthwhile activities while assessing their understanding of the concepts and processes of science, applications to technology, and ability to apply learning. In the two examples shown in Table 5.5, students are involved in activities that allow them to apply learning. Their performances provide evidence of what they know and are able to do.

EXAMPLE 5: Using Novelty to Extend Learning

Strategies: Role-play; design an action plan for researching a community problem; make suggestions and/or engage in community service to assist with the solution of the problem; share findings

Following the study of a science concept or principle, allow students to identify a problem or issue related to the local community. Some ideas are water usage, extinction of wildlife, air and air quality, health issues, energy sources or needs, transportation and energy issues, erosion or flooding, noise, urban expansion, and many others.

Students may assume the role of a newspaper or television investigative reporter. They should research the problem using a variety of resources, investigate the problem, identify the variables affecting the problem, and make suggestions for solving the problem. Students can write a newspaper article or give a radio or television news broadcast to share their findings.

Thought and Discussion

1. With a partner, identify a learning experience you have used or have seen used. Identify the strategies that are used in the learning experience. Suggest new and novel ways to structure the learning experience.

2. Design a notebook to enhance learning on an outdoor experience or field trip. Discuss some ways that out-of-classroom experiences can enhance learning.

VARYING STRATEGIES FOR DIVERSE LEARNERS

In some situations, students may be better served by varied assignments, tiered activities, contracts, centers, and/or other individualized or group methods of learning. With a rich supply of instructional resources and creative approaches, learning can be tailored to meet the needs of students, while, at the same time, helping students to assume more responsibility for their own learning.

Tiered Activities

Tiered activities have the same focus and objectives, but they provide different pathways for reaching the objectives. Strategies with varying degrees of difficulty are used to maximize the possibility that each student will learn concepts and skills and that each student will be appropriately challenged. Opportunities for relearning should be available through classroom learning centers, "take-home" activities, peer or adult tutoring, or direct instruction.

Contracts

For some students, a contractual arrangement may be useful. In this approach, action plans are developed by teachers and/or students that offer students choices in the ways they will learn key concepts and skills and in the ways they will show their learning.

Varying Activities

Within any instructional sequence or unit, methods, including expository, hands-on activity, demonstration, discussion, research, and open investigation, should vary according to student needs and interests to maximize learning. Interest and enrichment centers, models, manipulative materials and equipment, reference books, trade books, videotapes, Web sites, and other resources should be available for tiered learning and contractual approaches.

BEST PRACTICES IN SCIENCE EDUCATION

Best practices are a set of research-based approaches that are closely associated with high student achievement. Best practices may overlap with methods and strategies but provide additional insight into ways that methods and strategies can be used most effectively.

A list of best practices for the design and delivery of effective science is provided in the form of a checklist. The list can be useful when analyzing instructional materials for the ways they address important aspects of science or for analyzing instruction. Not all best practices will be found in a single unit, lesson, or classroom session.

CHECKLIST OF BEST PRACTICES

_____ Function as a facilitator of learning; guide and mediate the learning experience

_____ Provide a safe and supportive student-centered environment for learning

_____ Structure lessons to build on prior learning and lead to more complexity

_____ Use inquiry as a primary approach

_____ Use the vocabulary of science in communication

_____ Provide opportunities for students to ask inquiry questions and generate hypotheses

_____ Provide opportunities for students to plan investigations to test hypotheses

_____ Use manipulative materials to build/reinforce concepts

_____ Use cooperative, collaborative activity as opposed to competitive activity

_____ Use heterogeneous grouping and individualized instruction

_____ Use equipment, materials, and resources for multisensory learning

_____ Provide opportunities for students to develop logical reasoning and thinking skills

_____ Involve students in problem solving

_____ Use student-centered activities such as products and projects

_____ Use a variety of instructional resources and databases, simulations, and Web links

_____ Motivate and challenge students

_____ Use notebooks to organize thought and integrate writing

_____ Use appropriate technology (calculators, measurement tools, balances, computers)

_____ Use questions to engage students in discussions based on experiences and thought

_____ Apply learning to lives of students and to community, country, and global society

_____ Include connections to technology and explore technological design

_____ Devote time to reading books, nonfiction material, and current events

_____ Give responsibility to students for quality work, goal-setting, recordkeeping, monitoring evaluation, and so forth; empower students

_____ Give students choices (activities, resources, projects, research topics, partners, etc.)

_____ Give attention to affective needs and cognitive styles of learners; differentiate

_____ Model and practice principles of democracy and dispositions of science

Thought and Discussion

1. Discuss the relationship between methods, strategies, and best practices.

2. Identify one or more ways you can add "best practices" in your teaching. Design a plan to implement one or more best practices. Try it. Assess it. Report it.

Sample Activities for Primary/Intermediate and Middle/High School Science

Four sample activities are provided to demonstrate the application of methods, strategies, and best practices. Identify the ways methods, strategies, and best practices are used in each activity.

Activity One: Primary Grades: Discovering the Covering—Investigating Shells

Overview

Students are usually familiar with shells, especially if they have been to the ocean. But how many students know what shells really are? Shells appear to be nonliving objects that are part of the vast expanse of sand that makes up the beach. This activity will explore the properties of shells using the process skills of science and link these fascinating objects to the living organisms that created them.

Key Concepts

Objects have many observable properties, including size, shape, texture, color, magnetic properties, buoyancy, and mass. The properties can be measured using tools, such as rulers and balances.

Animals have different structures that serve different functions in growth, survival, and reproduction.

Instructional Objectives

Following this activity, students will:

- describe the physical properties of shells
- explain the ways they discovered the properties of color, texture, size and shape, mass, magnetic/nonmagnetic, and sink/float
- show an understanding of shells as structures of living organisms
- (optional) identify the name of one shelled animal and tell what they learned about it

Background Information

Students are most familiar with animals called vertebrates, those with backbones. But about 95 percent of all animals lack backbones and are called invertebrates. The phylum

Mollusca has seven classes and more than 100,000 known species of animals. Snails, oysters, clams, and octopuses are examples of mollusks. Mollusks are soft-bodied animals, most of which are protected by shells made of calcium carbonate. The soft bodies of mollusks have three parts: a muscular foot, a visceral mass containing internal organs, and a mantle, a fold of tissue that drapes over the visceral mass which may secrete a shell. Most mollusks have shells, but not all. Mollusks may live in terrestrial, aquatic, or marine habitats, with the latter being the most common.

The two largest classes of mollusks are the gastropods with single shells that spiral outward, such as snails, and the bivalves with two parts to their shells, such as clams and oysters.

Figure 5.2   Shells

Cone Snails   Clam Shells

SOURCE: www.nps.gov/calo/graphics/threeshells.jpg and www.nigms.nih.gov/.../sept02/images/shells.jpg

Shells are the exterior skeletons of mollusks that provide shape, protection, and possibly camouflage for the animal. Shells are made from the calcium the animals derive from their environment—from food or from water. Mollusks hatch from eggs with a tiny shell intact. The shell grows as the animal grows. Different species of mollusks make shells that are often unique to the species.

Some mollusks bury themselves in the sand like clams, and some crawl along the bottom of the ocean and eat plants and animals they find along the way. Still others attach themselves to rocks along the shore. Sometimes empty shells are inhabited by small crabs called hermit crabs.

Materials and Safety

For each group of four students—a set of shells with different properties; magnifiers; paper clips; string; balance and informal masses such as teddy bears, large paper clips, or chips; small tub of water; magnet

For the class—a set of shells with different properties (at least 2–3 for each of the students in the class, if possible); reference books and shell classification guides showing many different shells and pictures of the whole animal (shells and body parts): notebooks or data sheets

Inquiry Questions

What are the properties of shells? What kinds of animals have seashells? What is the function of the shell for the animal?

Engagement

1. Hold up a large shell and ask students what they think it is. Is the shell living or nonliving? What are its properties? Have students tell what they know about shells.

2. Ask students if they have ever collected shells? Where were they? Have them describe their experiences. For what are shells used? Do you have any shells in your home? Describe their use.

3. Many students may not realize that shells are parts of formerly living animals. Have a set of pictures of shelled animals available to show students or have one or more snails, clams, or oysters in their shells available for students to observe.

4. Ask students what they think the function of the shell is for the animal. Tell students that they will be investigating the properties of matter using shells and that during the investigation they should be thinking about what the function of the shell might be for the animal. Later in the investigation, students may find a picture of their shell, hopefully, with the soft part of the body exposed.

5. Ask students what questions they have about shells. Tell students they will investigate their questions about shells while investigating the properties of matter.

Exploration

1. Shells come in all shapes and sizes, and they will be used to investigate the properties of matter. Review the properties of matter: color, shape, size, texture, weight, magnetic property, and density (for primary grades, this means sink or float).

2. Each student will select one shell to study in detail. Students will follow the directions and record data on a data sheet to discover the properties of their shells.

   a. Observation: Use the magnifier to observe the color of the shell and any other unusual things you see with the magnifier. Are there any unusual marks on your shell? Draw your shell and record the properties. Turn your shell another way and draw it again.

   b. Shape: Is your shell most like: A circle? An oval? A square? A rectangle? A triangle?

   c. Measurement: Measure your shell with paper clips.

      How many paper clips long is your shell?

      How many paper clips wide is your shell?

      Take a piece of string and wrap it around your shell. How many paper clips does it take to go around your shell?

   d. Texture: Examine the texture of your shell. Is your shell rough or smooth? Form a group of four. Arrange the four shells from smoothest to roughest.

e. Similarities and differences: Identify one way that the four shells are alike and one way they are different. Record the ways.

f. Put the four shells on the balance. Use paper clips or other objects (or masses) to find the weight of the four shells.

g. Use the balance and weights to find the weight of your shell. In your group, order the shells from lightest to heaviest. Show the order in the boxes. Use the balance to help you order the shells from lightest to heaviest. Show the order.

h. Draw the outline of your shell on graph paper. Find the area covered by your shell by counting the number of boxes that are covered. Record the area.

i. Predict: Will your shell be attracted to a magnet? Test and record.

j. Predict: Will your shell sink or float in water? Test and record.

Explanation

Parts k, l, and m will prompt students to discuss procedures, describe properties, and investigate and discuss structure and function.

k. From a set of shells available in the classroom or on your table, select one that is most like yours and one that is different from yours. Draw the shell that is similar to yours and the one that is different from yours and explain the properties that make them similar and different.

l. Find a picture of your shell in one of the reference books. Find a picture of the shell with the body of the animal still intact. Draw the animal with its shell. Tell why you think the shell is important to the animal.

m. Write a sentence, story, or poem about your shell.

Evaluation

1. Describe the physical properties of your shell.

2. Explain how shells are alike and how they are different.

3. Describe one of the tests you did to discover the properties of your shell.

4. Explain what your shell was like as part of a living animal.

5. Describe the importance of shells to the animals that have them.

Elaboration and Extension

1. Research information about your mollusk. Where is it found? What does it eat? What is its life cycle like? What other interesting facts and information can you find?

2. Find pictures of shelled animals in their natural environments. Describe them. What is the economic value of shelled animals, such as clams, mussels, and oysters?

3. Write a sentence, a story, or a poem describing what life was like for the shelled animal. (Modified from J. Hillen, 1991, Sea shells are special, AIMS Newsletter.)

Activity Two: Intermediate–Middle Grades: Forensic Science—Investigating Fingerprints

Overview

Students will engage in an investigation to discover that fingerprints are unique to individuals. The inquiry investigation will provide a laboratory experience through which students will ask questions, collect and record data, share results, draw conclusions, and make generalizations. They will keep notebooks and research new questions.

Standards and Key Concepts

This activity provides basic information about the process of fingerprinting and its value in forensic science.

K–4: Characteristics of organisms

5–8: Structure and functions in living systems; diversity and adaptations of organisms; science in personal and social perspectives

In humans, fingerprints form before birth, and except for a few things that alter them, they remain unchanged throughout life.

Fingerprints provide evidence of human identity because every fingerprint is unique—even among identical twins. Fingerprints offer an infallible method of personal identification.

Instructional Objectives

Following this activity, students will:

- Describe the basic patterns of fingerprints
- Explain that fingerprints are unique to each individual (diversity)
- Describe how an individual can be identified by the patterns of their fingerprints
- Explain how fingerprints are used in forensic science

Background Information

What are fingerprints? Fingerprints are impressions of the raised surface of papillary skin (small projections) on the palm side of human fingers left on a surface when pressure is applied. Papillary skin is also present on the toes and bottoms of the feet. Palms, lower fingers, and soles of feet and toes are areas that provide unique impressions. Prints are identified and distinguished from one another by making quantitative and qualitative comparisons of the friction ridges. Slight differences may be detected by trained fingerprint examiners.

Fingerprints are kept in civil (police, military, public service) or criminal repositories and are used to determine if one has a criminal record or to verify a person's identity. In order to be useful, fingerprints must be distinct and clear of smudges.

Hands with ridge patterns were found in prehistoric writing, and in ancient China, thumb prints were found on clay seals. Fingerprint patterns—ridges, loops, and spirals—were mentioned in a 1686 treatise by Marcello Malpighi. Nine fingerprint patterns were discussed in the 1823 thesis of a professor of anatomy at the University of Breslau. Handprints were used by Sir William Hershel, chief magistrate of a district in India, in 1856 to seal contracts with the locals who believed that contact with the documents made it more binding.

In 1880, Dr. Henry Faulds recognized the importance of fingerprints as a means of identification and devised a system of classification. He published an article discussing fingerprints as a means of personal identification and a method for obtaining them.

In 1882, Gilbert Thompson of the United States Geologic Survey (USGS) used his fingerprints on a document to prevent forgery. In 1883, Mark Twain used fingerprints to identify a murderer in *Life on the Mississippi.* By 1892, after studying fingerprinting as a method of identification, the British anthropologist Sir Francis Galton published a book on the topic and included the first classification system for fingerprints. Galton calculated that the chances of two individual fingerprints being the same were 1 in 64 billion.

In 1901, Sir Edward Henry introduced the use of fingerprints for criminal identification and devised the Henry Classification System, which is still in use today.

Throughout the early 1900s, the use of fingerprints for personal identification grew among such organizations as the New York Civil Service Commission, New York State Prison System, St. Louis Police Department, Leavenworth Federal Prison, U.S. Army, U.S. Navy, U.S. Marine Corps, and law enforcement agencies.

Figure 5.3 shows three basic fingerprint patterns: arches, loops, and whorls. There are variations of these patterns.

Figure 5.3 Fingerprint Patterns

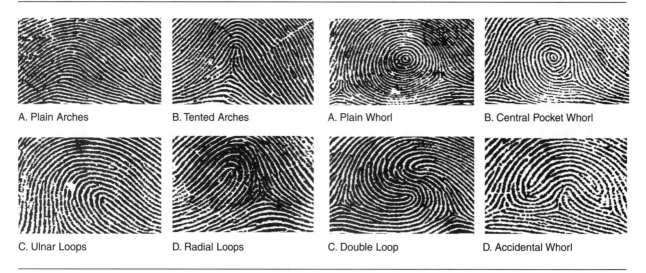

A. Plain Arches   B. Tented Arches   A. Plain Whorl   B. Central Pocket Whorl

C. Ulnar Loops   D. Radial Loops   C. Double Loop   D. Accidental Whorl

SOURCE: www.tpub.com/maa/12740_files/image582.jpg

Materials and Safety

Per student: one index card; one sheet of plain paper; #2 pencil; magnifier

Per group: transparent tape; a poster or transparency of fingerprint patterns or copies of the patterns

Per class: reference books on forensic science; access to additional information on fingerprinting, finger scanning, and so forth

Safety: Be sure to wash hands thoroughly after the activity

Inquiry Question

In what ways are human fingerprints similar and different? What are some ways the unique patterns of fingerprints can be used in society?

Engagement

1. You have undoubtedly heard of using fingerprints to identify missing persons or criminals. What do you know about fingerprints? Determine if students know that fingerprints are unique in almost every human being.

2. Use a magnifier to observe your fingerprints. What do you see? Observe the samples of arch, loop, and whorl shown on the poster or overhead transparency. With a partner, study the patterns and write a description for each pattern in your notebook.

3. In your notebook, write one or more questions you have about fingerprints.

Exploration

1. Make an outline of one hand on one side of a piece of plain paper and an outline of your other hand on the back side of the paper.

2. Take an index card and a soft pencil and make a "graphite pad" with the pencil. Build up the graphite until there is enough to coat a finger with gray dust.

3. Gently rub "pad" of a finger across the graphite. Place a piece of transparent tape across the graphite-covered finger and press gently so that the graphite transfers to the tape. Be sure to put the tape over the part of the finger where the pattern is most distinct.

4. Carefully transfer the piece of tape to the appropriate finger on the outline. Tape the print to the outline. Be careful not to "contaminate" the tape with other prints.

5. Repeat steps 3 and 4 for the other four fingers.

6. Use the magnifier and observe the pattern on each finger. Compare the pattern to the samples for arch, loop, and whorl and classify each of the fingerprints. Write A, L, or W above each of the fingers on the drawing.

7. Predict: Do you think the pattern of fingerprints on one hand will be the same on the other hand? Repeat the process with your other hand. Observe.

Explanation

1. Describe the pattern of fingerprints for your first hand.

2. Describe the pattern of fingerprints for your second hand. Are they the same? If not, how are they different?

3. Compare your patterns to others. What is the most common pattern? What is the least common?

4. Collect group or class data for each of the fingerprint patterns and graph the data.

5. What generalizations or conclusions can you make about fingerprints?

Evaluation

Use evidence from notebooks, discussion, activities, or other means to determine if students are able to:

1. Describe the basic patterns of fingerprints; identify similarities and differences in fingerprint patterns

2. Explain that fingerprints are unique to each individual

3. Describe how an individual can be identified by the patterns of his or her fingerprints

4. Explain how fingerprints are used in forensic science

Elaboration and Extension

1. In what ways is fingerprinting useful in forensic science? Read, research, or interview someone in law enforcement to learn more about the importance of fingerprints for identifying criminals. Share your findings.

2. What is a database of fingerprints? When and for what reasons do adults or children provide fingerprints? Do you think this is a good idea? Why or why not? Research the extent of the fingerprint database available for forensic science.

3. Where are other types of skin patterns found in humans? Are there toe patterns? Palm patterns? Investigate other patterns.

4. Read about finger scanning technology. What do you think about this innovation? Research similar technological innovations.

Application of Learning: Finger Scanning

Casinos in New Mexico, grocery stores in Texas, financial firms in New York, and the San Francisco International Airport use sensor or optical technology (called biometrics) that reads genetic material such as fingerprints, hands, irises and retinas in the eye, and faces for identification. A major school system in Philadelphia uses this type of technology to track thousands of workers.

How finger scanning works: A person types an identification code into a keypad and slides his or her index and middle fingers onto a small platform. The system takes a "picture" of the fingers, and the image is reduced to a binary number, which the system matches with the employee's database image. If they match, a green light glows, and the log-in is valid.

The system is highly accurate, and the information is totally different from the Federal Bureau of Investigation (FBI) database of fingerprints.

Finger scanning is an effective risk reduction tool and might become an effective security measure for schools. Research is being done to determine if this system might be useful for ensuring that students get on the right bus.

What is needed: privacy policies, assurance that the system is safe, and acceptance by teachers and the community. School officials see the process as an electronic version of the use of identification cards.

Activity Three: Middle–High School: Creating a Model of the Solar System

Overview

Models provide a means to visualize details of objects or relationships between objects. In this activity, students will make two models of the solar system: the first model will show the relative distances of the planets from the Sun, like a map; the second model will be a scale model of each of the planets and the Sun to show their relative sizes. There are three parts to the activity; thus, there will be three Explorations, each followed by an Explanation with questions for discussion.

Then, the three Explorations and Explanations will be followed by the Elaboration and Evaluation components to complete the activity.

You may want to design a context for the study. For example, students may assume the roles of astronomers working in a planetarium to design and create displays of the solar system for visitors, or they may be directors of a science center in a school system.

Standards and Key Concepts

Abilities Necessary to Do Scientific Inquiry: Student inquiries should culminate in formulating an explanation or model. Models should be physical, conceptual and mathematical. (NRC, 1996, p. 175)

The Earth is the third planet from the Sun in a system that includes the Moon, the Sun, eight other planets and their moons, and smaller objects, such as asteroids and comets.

The Sun, an average star, is the central and largest body in the solar system.

Models can be used to show characteristics of objects or show relationships between or among objects that cannot otherwise be seen easily or with the unaided eye.

As the complexity of any system increases, gaining an understanding of it depends increasingly on summaries, such as averages and ranges, and on descriptions of typical examples of that system. (AAAS, 1993, p. 278)

Materials and Safety

Per student: calculator; metric rulers or metric tape measure (optional: objects for comparisons: small sticky notes; staples; large and small paper clips)

Per class: several sheets of newspaper for comparison—lay 1½ single sheets side by side for approximate width of model; astronomy and picture books and resource materials (videotapes, computer software, Internet access)

Per group: one or two large sheets of newsprint or poster paper; markers or drawing pencils; drawing compass (optional: one package of clay)

Inquiry Question

How does a model of the solar system help to describe relative sizes and distances of the Sun and the planets and understand the size and complexity of the system?

Engagement

1. Ask students if they know how far away the Earth is from the Sun; from the nearest planet; from the farthest planet.

   • Students should investigate distances that are familiar, such as the distance across the United States; the distance around the Earth; the distance from a city in the United States to a city in another country. Have students report their findings in miles and in kilometers.

2. Ask students if they know the diameter of the Earth, the Sun, or any of the other planets. Is the Earth one of the smaller planets in the solar system or one of the larger planets?

3. Identify what students know and any misconceptions they have about relative sizes of planets and distances in the solar system.

4. Review metric measurement, if necessary.

- Millimeter (mm): 0.001 meter ~ diameter of a paper clip wire

- Centimeter (cm): 0.01 meter ~ a little more than the width of a small paper clip (about 0.4 inch)

- Kilometer (km): 1000 meters ~ somewhat further than ½ mile (about 0.6 mile)

Exploration #1: Finding the Distances of Planets From the Sun

To model the solar system, two scales will be considered, and students are asked to pick a scale where the distances from the planets to the Sun are small enough to fit on an open sheet of newspaper.

Scale 1: For the first scale, let 1 millimeter (mm) equal 1 astronomical unit (AU).
Have students identify 1 mm on the metric ruler or tape measure.

One astronomical unit is the average distance from the Sun to Earth.
1 AU = 150,000,000 kilometers

To convert kilometers (km) to millimeters using this scale, divide the distance of the planet from the Sun by 150,000,000 kilometers.

Example: Mercury is 58,000,000 kilometers from the Sun. Divide 58,000,000 kilometers by 150,000,000 kilometers per millimeter to get the number of millimeters Mercury is from the Sun in your scale model.

Ask students what the distance in mm will be: 58,000,000 km / 150,000,000 km per mm = 0.39 mm

On your scale model, Mercury will be 0.39 millimeter from the Sun, or 0.39 AUs.

Ask students why they think the number is less than 1. (The number is less than 1 because Mercury is closer to the Sun than Earth.)

Scale 2: For the second scale, let 1 millimeter equal 5,000,000 kilometers. Divide the planet's actual distance from the Sun by 5,000,000 kilometers.

Calculate the Earth's distance in mm using this scale.

Divide the Earth's distance from the Sun by 5,000,000 km per mm (150,000,000 km/ 5,000,000 km per mm = 3 mm). Ask students to share their findings.

Now, do the same for Mercury: Mercury is 58,000,000 kilometers from the Sun. Divide 58,000,000 kilometers by 5,000,000 kilometers per millimeter to get the number of millimeters Mercury is from the Sun in this second scale model.

Ask students what the distance in mm will be: 58,000,000 km / 5,000,000 km per mm = 11.6 mm

On this scale model, Mercury will be 11.6 millimeters from the Sun.

Complete the data table shown in Table 5.6. The numbers for Mercury have already been entered.

Table 5.6   Data Table

Planet	Distance from Sun in kilometers	Distance in mm Scale: 150,000,000 km (1 AU) = 1 mm	Distance in mm Scale: 5,000,000 km = 1 mm
Mercury	58,000,000	0.39	11.6
Venus	108,000,000		
Earth	150,000,000		
Mars	228,000,000		
Jupiter	780,000,000		
Saturn	1,431,000,000		
Uranus	2,877,000,000		
Neptune	4,510,500,000		
Pluto	5,916,000,000		

Explanation #1

1. Look carefully again at the numbers for Mercury, the closest planet to the Sun. Compare the distances in the two scales and give examples of objects that are about the size of the distance in mm of Mercury to the Sun for each scale (or find objects in the classroom that are about that size).

   - With 1 millimeter equal to 150,000,000 kilometers, Mercury is 0.39 millimeter from the Sun, less than half a millimeter, or about the width of a few hairs or a thin pencil line. With 1 millimeter equal to 5,000,000 kilometers, Mercury is 11.6 millimeters from the Sun or about the width of a large paper clip, a staple, or your smallest finger.

2. Compare the distances in the two scales for Pluto, the farthest planet from the Sun. Give examples of objects that are about the size of the distance in mm of Pluto to the Sun for each scale (or find objects in the classroom that are about that size.

   - When 1 millimeter equals 150,000,000 kilometers, Pluto is 39.4 millimeters from the Sun, about the width of a small sticky note or two adult fingers.

   - With 1 millimeter equal to 5,000,000 kilometers, Pluto is 1,183.2 millimeters from the Sun, a little longer than a meter stick.

3. Ask students to consider the two scales and determine which scale would be the most useful for making a model of the solar system that would be about the width of 1½ single pages of newspaper laid side by side.

   - A scale of 1 millimeter equal to 5,000,000 kilometers will work better for a model about the length of a meter stick.

4. Use the information in the table to make a scale model of the solar system marking the distances of the planets from the Sun.

Exploration #2: Finding the Diameters of the Sun and the Planets

Now that you have created a scale model for the distances of the planets to the Sun in the solar system, you will make scale models of the planets and the Sun. By doing this, you will be able to see their relative sizes.

1. For the sizes of the planets, you will try two different scales.

Scale 1: For the first scale, use 1 millimeter equals 50,000 kilometers.

Example: The Sun is 1,391,400 kilometers in diameter. Divide 1,391,400 kilometers by 50,000 kilometers per millimeter to get the diameter of the Sun in millimeters for this scale.

1,391,400 km / 50,000 km per millimeter = 27.8 millimeters
Using this scale, the Sun will be 27.8 millimeters in diameter.

Scale 2: For the second scale, use 1 millimeter equals 5,000 kilometers.

Example: The Sun is 1,391,400 kilometers in diameter. Divide 1,391,400 kilometers by 5,000 kilometers per millimeter to get the diameter of the Sun in millimeters for this scale.

1,391,400 km / 5,000 km per millimeter = 278.3 millimeters

On this scale model, the Sun will be 278.3 millimeters in diameter.

2. Complete the data table shown in Tabel 5.7. The numbers for the Sun have been entered.

Table 5.7   Data Table

Sun and Planets	Diameter in kilometers (km)	Diameter in mm Scale: 50,000 km = 1 mm	Diameter in mm Scale: 5,000 km = 1 mm
Sun	1,391,400	0.39	11.6
Mercury	4,878		
Venus	12,104		
Earth	12,756		
Mars	6,787		
Jupiter	142,800		
Saturn	120,660		
Uranus	50,800		
Neptune	48,600		
Pluto	3,100		

Explanation #2

1. Consider the diameters of the Sun and of the smallest planet, Pluto. If you were going to show these planets on the model you made showing relative distances, which scale would be more suitable? Give an example of an object that might be about the size of each diameter or find something in the classroom that is about each size.

- With 1 millimeter equal to 50,000 kilometers, the Sun would be about 28 mm or about the width of 1½ postage stamps. Pluto is 0.06 millimeter in diameter, so small a distance that it would hardly be visible on the model.

- With 1 millimeter equal to 5,000 kilometers, the Sun is 278 mm, almost the height of a sheet of notebook paper. Pluto is 0.62 millimeter in diameter, a little more than ½ millimeter, or the width of a human hair.

2. Given these distances, which scale would be more useful for making scale models of the planets and Sun? Why?

- A scale with 1 millimeter equal to 5,000 kilometers would be better because Pluto, the tiniest of the planets, would be visible on the model. You would be able to compare Pluto's size with the sizes of the other planets. With 1 millimeter equal to 50,000 kilometers, Pluto would not be visible.

Exploration #3: Making a Scale Model

Use the information on the table to draw or make scale models of the Sun and each of the planets. Start with the Sun so that you can see how all the other planets compare in size. Draw the diameter of the Sun and draw all or part of the Sun on the newsprint. Measure the diameter of each planet and show it at its appropriate distance from the Sun. Use a compass to complete a circle around the diameter, showing the size of the circular planet.

Option: Measure the diameter of each planet and make a three-dimensional model using modeling clay. Place each planet at the appropriate distance from the Sun.

Explanation #3

1. How does the Earth relate to the Sun and the other planets in distance and size?

2. Are any parts of the model surprising to you? If so, explain.

3. What does a model show that a set of numbers alone does not show? Find other models of the solar system in books or resource materials. Compare the models with your model. How are they alike and how are they different?

4. What new questions do you have about planet sizes and relative distances to the Sun?

Elaboration

1. Is the model you made suitable for a planetarium or museum? If not, what other scale might be used?

2. What other characteristics of the Sun and the planets might you want to include in a model for public display?

Evaluation

Write an explanation of the model as you would describe it to the visitors to the planetarium or museum.

Other evidence of student learning will be found in the data table calculations, answers to explanation questions, models made by students, and interviews with students throughout the activity.

Extension

1. Use books and resources to learn what is known about the planets and the other objects in the solar system and the ways that astronomers learned about the planets and other objects.

2. What are some of the challenges posed to scientists by the characteristics of the planets and heavenly bodies and their distances from the Earth?

3. Design a research project for learning more about one or more planets or other objects in the solar system. Plan a presentation for your class and be sure to include visuals in your project.

Completed Tables

Table 5.8   Distances of the Planets From the Sun

Planet	Distance From Sun in kilometers	Distance in mm Scale: 150,000,000 km (1 AU) = 1 mm	Distance in mm Scale: 5,000,000 km = 1 mm
Mercury	58,000,000	0.39	11.6
Venus	108,000,000	0.72	21.6
Earth	150,000,000	1.0	30
Mars	228,000,000	1.52	45.6
Jupiter	780,000,000	5.2	156
Saturn	1,431,000,000	9.54	286.2
Uranus	2,877,000,000	19.2	575.4
Neptune	4,510,500,000	30.1	902.1
Pluto	5,916,000,000	39.4	1183.2

Table 5.9   Diameters of the Sun and Planets

Sun and Planet	Diameter in kilometers (km)	Diameter in Scale: 50,000 km = 1 mm	Diameter in Scale: 5,000 km = 1 mm
Sun	1,391,400	27.83	278.3
Mercury	4,878	0.10	0.976
Venus	12,104	0.24	2.4
Earth	12,756	0.26	2.6
Mars	6,787	0.14	1.4

Sun and Planet	Diameter in kilometers (km)	Diameter in Scale: 50,000 km = 1 mm	Diameter in Scale: 5,000 km = 1 mm
Jupiter	142,800	2.86	28.6
Saturn	120,660	2.41	24.1
Uranus	50,800	1.02	10.2
Neptune	48,600	0.98	9.8
Pluto	3,100	0.06	0.62

Activity Four: Experiment for Middle School–High School Level—Eggs-actly Osmosis

Overview

This experiment will allow students to perform a controlled experiment. The activity, although engaging, takes care and patience to provide the data needed to observe change.

Chicken eggs are cells. Decalcified eggs are raw eggs without their shells. The material inside the egg is held together by the tough membrane that is under the shell. Although it is tough, it can be broken. The decalcified egg should be handled gently. With that precaution, students should have a great time exploring osmosis.

Key Concepts

5–8: Cells carry on the many functions needed to sustain life. They grow and divide, thereby producing more cells. This requires that they take in nutrients, which they use to provide energy for the work that cells do and to make materials that a cell or an organism needs. (NSES, 1996)

9–12: Cells have particular structures that underlie their functions. Every cell is surrounded by a membrane that separates it from the outside world. Inside the cell is a concentrated mixture of thousands of different molecules that form a variety of specialized structures that carry out such cell functions as energy production, transport of molecules, waste disposal, synthesis of new molecules, and the storage of genetic material. (NRC, 1996)

Instructional Objectives

Through this activity, students will:

- conduct a controlled experiment to test the process of osmosis under two different conditions
- explain what happens during the process of osmosis and infer why it happens in the environments tested
- identify and describe the types and treatments of variables in a controlled experiment including the manipulated variable (independent), the responding variable (dependent), the controlled variables, and the uncontrolled variables
- explain their procedures, observations and measurements, data, and findings
- apply their learning to the functioning of cells in the human body

Background Information

Osmosis is a special kind of diffusion; it is the diffusion of water across a semipermeable membrane. Water molecules diffuse freely across membranes. Water moves from an area of greater concentration to an area of lesser concentration. The movement of water across cell membranes and the balance of water between a cell and its environment are crucial to the functioning of the cell. The diffusion of water across a membrane generates a pressure called osmotic pressure. Osmosis is of great importance in biological processes where the solvent is water. The transport of water and other molecules across biological membranes is essential to many processes in living organisms.

Osmosis occurs from an area of high concentration of water molecules to an area of low concentration of water molecules. In osmosis, it is only water that moves in the following directions:

- From a region of high water concentration to a region of low water concentration
- From a weaker solution (because it has more water) to a stronger one (less water)

The environment that surrounds the cell determines the direction in which the water molecules move. When cells are in an environment where the solution outside the cell is equal in concentration to their cytoplasm (within the cell), the cell will remain the same size and shape. If the concentrations are different, the cells could shrink from loss of water or burst with too much.

Figure 5.4   Osmosis

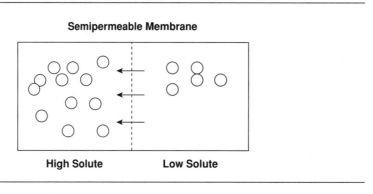

Cell membranes are completely permeable to water; therefore, the environment the cell is exposed to can have a significant effect on the cell.

A hypertonic solution contains a high concentration of solute relative to another solution, such as the cell's cytoplasm. When a cell is placed in a hypertonic solution, water moves out of the cell, causing the cell to shrivel.

A hypotonic solution contains a low concentration of solute relative to another solution. When a cell is placed in a hypotonic solution, water moves into the cell, causing the cell to swell and possibly explode.

Isotonic solutions contain the same concentration of solute as another solution. When a cell is placed in an isotonic solution, the water diffuses into and out of the cell at the same rate. The fluid that surrounds human body cells is isotonic.

Materials and Safety

Per team: three decalcified eggs (eggs that have been soaked in vinegar 1 to 2 days to dissolve shells); vinegar solution from the decalcified eggs; three wide-top plastic cups or 400 mL beakers; Karo syrup; metric measuring tape; balance (and mass set); distilled water; paper towels; clock or timer; student notebooks

Safety and Care: Care should be taken when using glass beakers; students should exercise caution when working with decalcified eggs because they break easily. The decalcified egg is very fragile and is held together with only the thin membrane around the egg. If an egg is broken, the data for that egg will be useless.

Inquiry Questions

What will be the effect on the amount of water inside of an egg (based on the changes in mass or size of the egg) when the egg is placed in a new environment of (1) distilled water or (2) corn syrup? What will the data show about the process of osmosis in these two situations?

Engagement

Find out what students know about diffusion and osmosis. Review cell structure and the function of the cell membrane.

Ask thought-provoking questions, such as why would a person stranded on a desert island die more quickly from drinking salt water than by drinking no water at all? Other questions related to osmosis and the human body may be asked to create interest.

Tell students they are going to study osmosis by putting decalcified eggs into two different environments to observe what happens. (A third egg may be kept in the original vinegar solution that decalcified the eggs as a "control.") Introduce the inquiry questions.

In this experiment, students will observe what happens to the amount of water inside a decalcified egg (as determined by its mass and size) when it is placed in a new environment. One egg will be placed in distilled water and the other in corn syrup to discover what happens to each egg over time.

Measurements will be taken at various intervals. It is important that students handle the eggs very carefully so that they do not break at any time during the experiment. Students will be working with the eggs for approximately 30 minutes and handling them several times. Reinforce that it is very important to have accurate timing, measurement, and recording throughout this experiment.

Ask students to predict what will happen to the mass and size of decalcified eggs when they are placed in corn syrup and in distilled water. Students should use notebooks for recording predictions, procedures, observations, data, and all other components of the experiment.

Exploration

1. Set two decalcified eggs on a paper towel. Make and record any observations.

2. Using a balance, find the mass of each of two decalcified eggs. Record the mass in grams for each egg on the data table under "mass in g at 0 minutes."

Figure 5.5   Measuring on a Balance

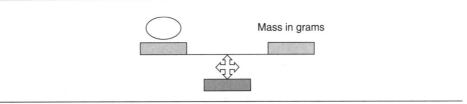

3. Using the tape measure, measure the circumference of each egg around its center. Record the circumference of each egg in centimeters on the data table under "circumference in cm at 0 minutes."

Figure 5.6   Measuring Circumference

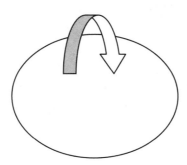

4. Keep another decalcified egg in the vinegar solution. Have one group find its mass and circumference at the beginning and at the end of the experiment. Compare the results from the eggs in distilled water and in corn syrup to the egg in vinegar (the control) at the end of the experiment. Record your measurements in Table 5.10.

Table 5.10   Data Table

Egg #	Mass g at 0 min	Mass g at 10 min	Mass g at 20 min	Mass g at 30 min	Circumference cm at 0 min	Circumference cm at 10 min	Circumference cm at 20 min	Circumference cm at 30 min
#1 in distilled water								
#2 in syrup								
#3 in vinegar (control)								

Beginning Time #1:   Ending time after 10 minutes:

Beginning Time #2:   Ending time after 10 minutes:

Beginning Time #3:   Ending time after 10 minutes:

5. Put distilled water in one cup; put corn syrup in a second cup. Put enough liquid to cover an egg, but be aware that the liquid level will rise when the egg is put into the cup. Be ready to time the experiment as soon as the eggs are placed into the cups. Carefully place an egg in the cup with distilled water; place another egg in the cup with corn syrup. Record the starting time of your experiment and begin timing 10 minutes.

6. After 10 minutes gently remove the eggs from the cups or beakers and lay them on a paper towel. Blot them dry on the paper towels; then measure the mass and circumference of each egg. Record the measurements in the data table for 10 minutes. Return the eggs to the cups and record the time. Begin timing 10 minutes.

7. Repeat the procedure for removing eggs from cups, finding mass and size, and record data after 20 minutes and after 30 minutes.

8. After 30 minutes, analyze your data to determine if or how the eggs in the distilled water, corn syrup, and vinegar changed. Write a summary of the experiment in your notebook and describe your findings.

9. Share your data with other groups. Collect data from five other groups and record the data in Table 5.11. Look for patterns. Write a summary statement for the findings from six groups in your notebook.

Table 5.11   Data

Group #	Distilled Water				Syrup			
	0	**10**	**20**	**30**	**0**	**10**	**20**	**30**
1								
2								
3								
4								
5								

10. Based on data from all groups, draw a conclusion about what happened to the eggs in distilled water and corn syrup over time. What do you think will happen to them if left in the new "environments" for a longer period of time?

   (Optional: Return your eggs to the cups and leave them for 12–24 hours or more. Measure, record, and discuss findings.)

Explanation

1. Why do you think the shells had to be removed from the eggs prior to doing this experiment?

2. Describe the procedures you used for this experiment in terms of the variables.

   • What was the responding (dependent) variable?

   The change in mass and size of the egg.

   • What was the manipulated (independent) variable?

   The environment that you created to see how it would affect the mass and size of the egg.

   • What variables did you control throughout the experiment?

   One environment was kept as a "control" to show what would happen to the egg if left in the same environment (no treatment).

   Other variables that were controlled by the researchers were cups, amount of time in solution, amount of material in the cup, way the eggs were handled, amount of distilled water or corn syrup on the eggs when weighing. (Both eggs were blotted.)

3. Describe the importance of controlling the variables in an experiment. Explain how your experiment would be different if you did not control the variables.

4. Describe your data. Did the mass or size of the eggs change in the new environments? If so, how did they change? How did they compare to the egg that was left in the vinegar?

5. What conclusion did you draw from your data? Is your conclusion from group data similar to or different from the conclusion drawn from your group data? Explain.

   • Discrepant data can lead to discussion of procedures, care and accuracy of measurement, and other issues related to conducting experiments. If necessary, students may conduct experiments again at home or at a center in the classroom.

6. Explain your findings in terms of the process of osmosis.

   • This experiment shows that water moved from an area of greater concentration to lesser concentration through the eggs' membranes. There was a greater concentration of water **outside** the egg for the egg in distilled water. Therefore, the egg should have gained mass and size since water moved into the egg.

   • There was a greater concentration of water **inside** the egg in corn syrup. Therefore, the egg should have lost mass and size as water passed through the membrane to the corn syrup.

   • There should have been no or very little change in the mass or size of the egg in the vinegar.

Evaluation

Through a number of assessment measures, students should show their understanding of the need for identifying and controlling variables in experiments that are testing the effects of one variable on another.

After 16 hours, the mass of the egg in distilled water was 91 grams and the circumference was 16.1 cm. The egg in corn syrup had a mass of 49 grams and a circumference of 12 cm. Are these the data consistent with what you learned about osmosis? Explain why or why not. Students should apply what they learned about osmosis through their experiment to explain this (and other) phenomena.

Students should be able to explain the process of osmosis and relate it to the functioning of cells in the human body.

Table 5.12   Sample Data for Osmosis

Egg #	Mass g at 0 min	Mass g at 10 min	Mass g at 20 min	Mass g at 30 min	Circumference cm at 0 min	Circumference cm at 10 min	Circumference cm at 20 min	Circumference cm at 30 min
#1 in distilled water	80g	90g	91g	91g	15.8cm	15.9cm	15.8cm	15.9cm
#2 in syrup	87g	85g	82g	89g	15.8cm	15.5cm	15.5cm	15cm
#3 in vinegar (control)	89g			89g	15.8cm			15.8cm

Elaboration and Extensions

1. What will happen to a decalcified egg that is put into a saltwater solution? Will the egg lose mass and size or gain mass and size? Predict. Try it. Put 3 teaspoons of salt in the water in the cup. Observe what happens. Apply what you have learned to explain your findings. What new questions do you have?

2. How do cell membranes function in the human body to regulate what goes into and out of cells? What type of environment is necessary for body cells to maintain their shape and size?

3. Osmosis occurs because of a difference in solute concentrations of two solutions. The differences can be defined as **isotonic**—the solutions being compared have equal concentrations of solutes; **hypertonic**—the solution with a higher concentration of solutes; and **hypotonic**—the solution with the lower concentration of solutes. Red blood serum is an isotonic solution for red blood cells. This means that both the cytoplasm in the cell and the serum surrounding the cell have equal concentrations of solute. Red blood cells have a disk shape. Predict what you think will happen to the shape of red blood cells that are placed into a (a) hypertonic solution and (b) hypotonic solution.

   • Explanation: A hypertonic solution contains a high concentration of solute relative to another solution, such as the cell's cytoplasm. When a cell is placed in a hypertonic solution, the water moves out of the cell, causing the cell to shrivel.

   • A hypotonic solution contains a low concentration of solute relative to another solution. When a cell is placed in a hypotonic solution, the water enters the cell, causing the cell to swell and possibly explode.

   • Isotonic solutions contain the same concentration of solute as another solution. When a cell is placed in an isotonic solution, the water diffuses into and out of the cell at the same rate. The fluid that surrounds human body cells is isotonic.

4. The liquid portion of the blood, the plasma, is a complex solution containing more than 90 percent water. The water of the plasma is freely exchangeable with that of body cells

and other extracellular fluids and is available to maintain the normal state of hydration of all tissues.

What might happen if your blood plasma changed chemically? How would a change in osmotic pressure affect the blood cells?

5. Research how osmosis applies to water purification and desalination, waste material treatment, and other chemical and biochemical laboratory and industrial processes.

Thought and Discussion

1. Analyze each of the sample activities. Identify the key concepts, process and thinking skills, and dispositions that are addressed through each of the sample activities.

2. How would the teacher's depth of understanding of the concepts aid in facilitating the activities?

3. What are some ways to provide for relearning in the event a child did not grasp the concepts from the activity or for extended learning for students who grasped concepts?

4. How would additional resources and materials allow teachers to differentiate instruction? Give examples related to one or more of the sample activities.

5. How does the consistent format for the activities help teachers to interpret the activities? In what ways does a consistent format inform the instructional process? What other benefits does the consistent format provide?

6. Create a student data sheet for one or more of the activities.

7. Note the interdisciplinary nature of the activities. Identify goals and standards from other subject areas and the ways concepts and skills from these areas were included. Discuss the advantages of addressing multiple goals and standards in one activity.

Revisit the Initial Question

What methods, strategies, and best practices will enhance the quality of the curriculum and strengthen the instructional process?

6

Tools for Thinking and Meaning

How does the use of questions, graphic organizers, links to technology and society, and notebooks enhance the teaching/learning process and contribute to high quality instruction?

QUESTIONS

The use of questions, cues, and advance organizers is linked positively to increased student achievement (Marzano et al., 2001).

Horizon Research (Weiss et al., 2003) identified the use of questioning strategies as an indicator of the high quality classroom. Yet, the results of this study showed that this indicator was observed in only 16 percent of over 350 classrooms participating in the study.

As with all skills, teachers must practice the art of asking good questions in the context of science, and thought-provoking questions should be an integral part of the instructional plan. Questions may be added as the lesson evolves, but a core set of questions written into the plan will ensure that students have the opportunity to think critically and logically throughout the inquiry process. Questions will also help to keep the lesson focused and provide important feedback about student learning.

Some questions that evoke thinking in students are shown in two organizational patterns. Table 6.1 shows questions at various levels of thought. Table 6.2 shows another way to organize questions—according to types of inquiry tasks.

Table 6.1   Questions at Various Levels of Thought

Level of Thought	Questions
Knowledge: identification and recall of information; define terms; knowledge of criteria	• Who, what, when, where, how? • What is the definition of this term? • How would you use this piece of equipment? • Who invented the microscope?
Comprehension: organize or select facts or ideas; interpret ideas; translate—make estimates or predictions based on conditions; can use an abstraction when its use is given	• What are some examples of this concept? • In what way(s) can you classify these objects or ideas? • Based on what you know now, what do you think will happen next? • What instrument(s) can you use to find the mass of the object?
Application: use of theory, principles, ideas, or methods to solve a problem; use an abstraction correctly in a new situation	• What are some ways you can apply this concept or principle to your life? To your environment? • Can you design a product that uses this principle? • Can you explain why _____ happened?
Analysis: breaks down material into component parts; detection of relationships of the parts and of the way they are organized	• How are the criteria similar to and different from your sample? • How is _____ similar to or different from ____? • What is the cause/effect relationship here? • How would you describe the relationships between concepts shown on a diagram or graphic organizer? • How do the data you collected support your hypothesis? How do your data compare to others? What data are relevant to the problem? • What trends are shown on the graph?
Synthesis: putting together of elements from many sources and parts to form	• How would you teach this concept to another? • Can you create a useful model from these components?

Level of Thought	Questions
a whole; involves some uniqueness or originality in design of a new pattern or structure	• Can you invent a new product? • What are some different ways you can test this hypothesis? • Can you analyze data and trends and design an action plan for learning more about a problem or issue or for solving a problem?
Evaluation: making of judgments about the value of ideas, works, solutions, methods, and so forth; using criteria and (internal or external) standards for appraising	• What criteria would you use to assess ____? • How will this plan help you to meet the standards we are trying to reach? • What methods were the most effective? • What score would you give this product or plan and why? • Why were some of the proposed solutions to the problem faulty?

Table 6.2   Questions Related to Types of Inquiry

Types of Inquiry	Questions
Investigations	• What evidence or prior knowledge do you have? • What do you need to know? • What is your question? What are some ways you might investigate this question? • What is your hypothesis? • What data do you need to collect? How will data be organized? • What observations did you make? • What process did you or will you use? • What types of technology, equipment, and resources did you use? • Are the data providing the evidence you need to answer the inquiry question? • Were the data consistent? What do they show? What relationships did you discover? • What did you learn? • How will you link new learning to prior knowledge? • Did you answer the inquiry question? • In what ways can you apply your learning? • What connections can you make to your life? To technology and society?
Decision-Making or Problem-Solving Tasks	• What is the problem? What is the decision? • What procedures will give you the data you need? Describe your approach. • What procedures or tests will need to be conducted to collect the data you need? • How much data will you need to solve the problem or make the decision?

(Continued)

Table 6.2 (Continued)

Types of Inquiry	Questions
	• What materials and resources will you need? • What problems might you encounter? • Can you differentiate between fact and opinion? • Can you support your decision with data? What is one solution to the problem? • What are the trade-offs to the solution? • Are there other solutions?
Inventions	• What will the invention do? • What scientific principles will be applied? • How will the model be constructed? • How will your invention be an improvement over others? • What are some designs that might be used? • Are some materials better than others for this product? Can you create a similar product from different materials? • What resources can provide information for this project? • How were you able to achieve your goal? • What did you learn from this experience that will help you better understand technology and technological design?
Defend a Position	• What is your current belief? • What are the conflicting beliefs that others have? • How does this issue or problem affect you emotionally? Economically? Personally? • What information do you have to support your beliefs? • What is the difference between fact and opinion? • What questions do you or others have? • What further research will you do? • What data will you need to collect and record? • What are some ways you can acquire new data to support your position? • What new evidence or data did you find? How have your ideas changed? • What argument and data will you use to defend your position? • What questions still remain?

Thought and Discussion

Give an example to show how questions can be used to:

Motivate students

Engage students

Foster creativity

Develop critical thinking skills

Develop logical thought processes

Enhance concept understanding

GRAPHIC ORGANIZERS

Students may be challenged to create graphic organizers to show the ways they frame thought, link new learning to prior learning, and make connections to their lives, technology, and society. Research prepared by the Institute for the Advancement of Research in Education (Inspiration Software, Inc., 2003) identified 29 scientifically based research studies that support the use of graphic organizers for improving student learning and performance across grade levels with diverse students in a broad range of content areas.

There are many types of graphic organizers, and a few basic structures are shown here. There are at least six ways of organizing knowledge to show the relationships between concepts or between concepts and events. Graphic organizers are powerful tools for creating mental models that aid the learner in retaining and recalling information.

Figures 6.1 to 6.6 show one or two examples for each of six basic structures in the context of elementary science. The types of relationships displayed are:

- descriptive: a main idea at the center with subcategories or properties radiating from the center that sometimes include "linking words" to identify relationships
- sequential: used to show a logical sequence of events, as a flowchart or time line
- process/causal: used to show cause and effect relationships
- categorical: a horizontal or vertical treelike configuration used for classification
- comparison/relational: identifies similarities and differences or comparisons between two or more objects or events
- problem/solution: used to show thinking about a problem by identifying plausible solutions

Figure 6.1   Descriptive: State the concept and identify features that help describe it and/or show unique properties.

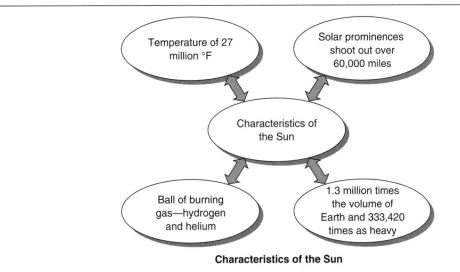

Characteristics of the Sun

Figure 6.2   Sequence or Time Line: Events listed in chronological order.

Example #1

Significant Events in the History of Medicine, 1800–1900

1801	Edward Jenner conquered deadly smallpox
1846	William Norton used ether for painless surgery
1854	Florence Nightingale stressed the importance of hygiene in preventing disease
1861	Louis Pasteur used a microscope to discover dangerous bacteria
1869	Joseph Lister used carbolic acid as an antiseptic during surgery to prevent infection
1895	Wilhelm Roentgen discovers the X-ray

Example #2

Significant Events in the History of Space Exploration

1981	1983	1986	1988	1994
First U.S. space shuttle launched; John Young and Robert Crippen	Dr. Sally Ride: First woman in space; mission specialist on STS-7, launched from Kennedy Space Center, Florida, on June 18, 1983.	*Challenger* explosion kills seven astronauts and one teacher	*Discovery* becomes first shuttle launched after *Challenger* accident	Scientists find black hole using Hubble Telescope

Figure 6.3   Process/Causal: Identify the stages in a process to show cause and effect.

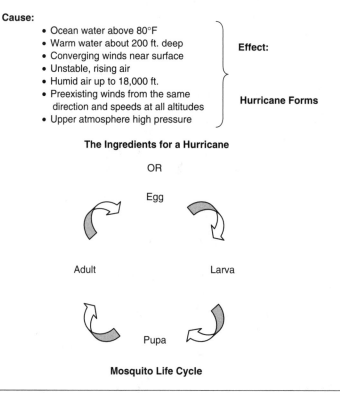

Cause:
- Ocean water above 80°F
- Warm water about 200 ft. deep
- Converging winds near surface
- Unstable, rising air
- Humid air up to 18,000 ft.
- Preexisting winds from the same direction and speeds at all altitudes
- Upper atmosphere high pressure

Effect:

Hurricane Forms

The Ingredients for a Hurricane

OR

Egg

Adult

Larva

Pupa

Mosquito Life Cycle

Figure 6.4 Concept Categories: Identify subcategories of big ideas or constructs and show relationships; may include descriptions.

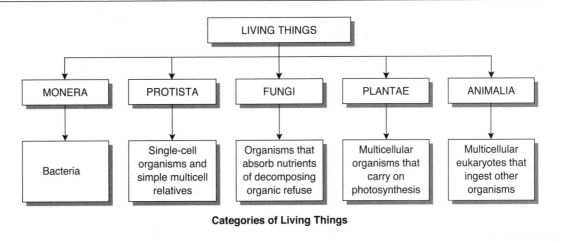

Categories of Living Things

Figure 6.5 Comparison/Relational: Show similarities and differences between two or more objects or events; identify properties that are shared and those that are unique.

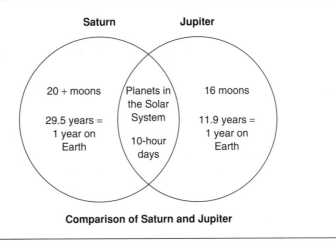

Comparison of Saturn and Jupiter

Figure 6.6 Problem/Solution: Identify problems, conduct research, and show possible or plausible solutions.

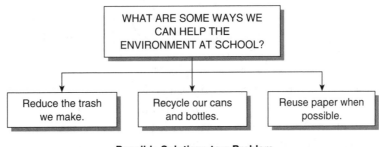

Possible Solutions to a Problem

Thought and Discussion

1. Select a science topic you teach (or know well) and identify a minimum of three key concepts related to the topic. Create a graphic organizer using any one of the six types shown previously.

    a. Re-create the graphic on chart paper and post the chart on the wall. Be ready to explain how the graphic shows the relationship between concepts.

    b. (Optional Strategy: In a large group, conduct a gallery walk allowing a short time at each graphic so that small groups may view and discuss each sample of work.)

2. Consider what you needed to know to be able to design your graphic. Work backward and consider:

    a. What experiences and types of learning were necessary for you to create the graphic?

    b. What organizational and thinking skills did you use in the process of creating the graphic?

3. How can the use of graphic organizers help students to organize and retain knowledge?

SCIENCE, TECHNOLOGY, AND SOCIETY

Review definitions of science, technology, and society:

-   Science provides explanations for observations about the natural world.
-   Technology is the application of the principles of science; the many ways humans apply science to enrich and improve their lives.
-   Society is the world in which the student lives as well as the expanded global community.

One of the primary goals of studying the relationships between science, technology, and society is the development of an informed citizenry capable of making wise decisions about both science and technology and acting on those decisions in a responsible manner.

The advancement of technology is dependent on creativity of thought and design; understanding of materials and resources; model building; the functioning, durability, and practicality of products; and a clear understanding of the trade-offs (environmental, economic, social, health/hazard, emotional) to the society that are associated with the development, implementation, and use of technology, among other things.

Throughout the elementary, middle, and secondary grades, students will investigate many concepts and principles that are new to them. The content at every grade level is an important component of the K–12 sequence, offering one of many building blocks needed to reach greater understanding of big ideas over time. It is critical that concepts are applied not only to technology and society as a community, but also to the lives of students and others as individual members of society.

When connections are made to the nature and history of science, career areas, and other areas of the curriculum, students are able to see the unity and relevance of knowledge, and there is a greater chance that learning will become a part of the long-term memory system.

Planning guides may be used to show connections. When general headings are used, there are opportunities to show different types of connections. For example, consider the three-column guide in Table 6.3:

- column one shows the unit title and standards-related concepts
- column two shows direct connections, that is, those connections or applications of the concepts to classroom practice and to the lives of students
- column three shows connections to local, state, national, and global environments and identifies related problems and issues that may be of interest to students for research or extended study

Table 6.3   Planning Guide for Linking Science to Technology and Society

Unit of Study and Key Concepts	Technology and Applications	Local, State, National, and Global Connections or Problems/Issues
Unit: Weather **Concepts:** The Sun provides the light and heat necessary to maintain the temperature of the Earth. Thermometers and other instruments are used to gather information about weather.	**Technology:** Students use instruments at a weather station. **Applications:** Students watch the weather channel on television. Students make clothing choices based on weather. Disaster drills related to severe weather are practiced periodically.	Meteorologists use Doppler radar and satellites to gather and interpret information and predict weather. Severe weather—tornados and hurricanes—can have devastating effects on communities. How is technology helping meteorologists to understand and predict severe weather? How does weather-related damage to crops affect the economy annually? What are the various careers in meteorology?

NOTEBOOKS

Notebooks as Tools for Learning

Using a science notebook throughout inquiry investigations helps to focus attention on the processes of science, as well as important concepts. Many science programs have activities that include student data sheets, which vary but include inquiry questions, data tables and graphs, questions for processing information, and resources.

Students may use notebooks to record predictions, describe action plans, record observations, collect data, summarize findings, and create written and visual explanations to show understanding of science concepts. Notebooks may also include summaries of articles, Web searches, research, essays, and stories that complement the classroom work.

Table 6.4 Notebook Entries and Their Descriptions

Notebook Entries	Descriptions of Entries
Inquiry Question; Problem or Purpose of Investigation	• Question and/or problem written in student's words • Work is clear and concise • Worthy question or problem relates to "key" concepts
Prediction	• Connects to prior experience or knowledge • Need not be "correct" but should show thought • Prediction is clear and reasonable; relates to questions • Student gives an explanation or reason
Action Plan and/or Procedures for Investigation	• Plan is reasonable and relates to question • Describes a clear sequence of events and directions • States materials needed • Identifies variables: manipulated, responding, controlled • Designs and uses data organizer(s)
Data/Observations	• Relate to question and plan; well-organized and accurate • Includes words, drawings, charts, graphs, numbers, and so forth
Conclusions	• Identify the "aha" and/or observations and insights • Clear statements of findings; describes in own words • Link to inquiry question, procedure, and data or evidence • Include reflective thought • Make connections to personal life, technology, and society
Next Steps/ Formulating New Questions	• Include student generated ideas and new questions worthy of research • Add extensions and applications of original inquiry question; may include reading, interview, Internet, or other research • May include an action plan for further study
Student Reflections	• Identify science content, process skills, and dispositions embedded in activities • Link science to math, language arts, social studies, and other areas of the curriculum • Describe learning in relation to the context • Show evidence of understanding of relevance of learning

Inquiry-centered science programs that emphasize the use of student notebooks have been found to increase the language proficiency test scores as well as science achievement test scores of participating students. Scores on state-mandated science tests also showed significant gains for these students (Klentschy et al., 2001).

Notebook entries will not necessarily be the same for all activities. Notebook pages can be designed by teachers to capture evidence of learning. At a more advanced level, notebook entries can be determined by students prior to the investigation. Table 6.4 identifies various types of entries that may be included in a notebook and briefly describes each type of entry.

Thought and Discussion

Select a sample activity from this book or one that you use in your classroom. Design a notebook page to use with the activity.

Discuss:

1. How will the notebook help to guide the instructional process and direct students?

2. What evidence of student learning will be captured in the notebook?

3. How will the notebook show evidence of student thinking?

4. In what ways will the notebook allow you to integrate instruction?

5. What other value will the notebook provide?

Revisit the Initial Question

How does the use of questions, graphic organizers, links to technology and society, and notebooks enhance the teaching/learning process and contribute to high quality instruction?

7

Assessments to Guide Instruction

How do carefully crafted assessments improve the quality of teaching and enhance student learning?

ASSESSMENTS AS TOOLS FOR LEARNING

Assessment is an important part of the standards-based curriculum. Valid assessments that link directly to the state and local instructional goals and standards provide continuous feedback to both teachers and students about the learning of valued concepts and skills. This connection of assessments to goals and standards is particularly important when state standards are used as the basis for statewide testing and other norm referenced measures of student learning.

Figure 7.1 shows the relationships of curriculum and instruction to state and local standards and standards-based (state) assessments. The graphic provides a vision for standards-based learning and highlights the importance of high quality curriculum and instruction for preparing students to be successful on standards-based assessments.

Classroom assessment plays a critical role in monitoring and guiding learning. Students who do not show evidence of learning on informal classroom assessments may be given additional opportunities to learn important concepts. For example, centers might be designed to provide resource materials, additional hands-on activities, videotapes, or Web sites for relearning concepts.

Students who show exceptional aptitude and interest or are quick to grasp concepts may extend their learning by visiting Web sites, conducting survey or experimental research, exploring careers, and planning projects. They should be given time to share their work with other interested students.

Figure 7.1   The Relationship of Curriculum and Instruction to Standards and Standards-Based Assessments

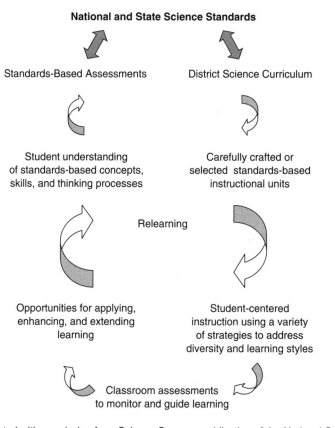

National and State Science Standards

Standards-Based Assessments

District Science Curriculum

Student understanding of standards-based concepts, skills, and thinking processes

Carefully crafted or selected standards-based instructional units

Relearning

Opportunities for applying, enhancing, and extending learning

Student-centered instruction using a variety of strategies to address diversity and learning styles

Classroom assessments to monitor and guide learning

Reprinted with permission from Science Scope, a publication of the National Science Teachers Association, 1840 Wilson Boulevard, Arlington, VA 22201-3000.

Thought and Discussion

Identify the relationships shown in Figure 7.1. Summarize the implications for successful teaching and learning.

DESIGNING ASSESSMENTS

Accountability for student learning implies that there is evidence to show what students know and are able to do related to the instructional goals and standards. An assessment package that has multiple and varied ways to gather information about student learning is an important component of the high quality curriculum.

Good classroom assessments should promote learning, be interesting, motivate students, and be part of daily instruction. Carefully constructed assessments are able to provide:

- opportunities for students to show what they know and can do in a variety of ways
- evidence of student thinking and problem solving
- evidence of skill development and dispositions

Research in classroom assessment confirms that frequent feedback to students regarding their progress in reaching learning goals and standards increases student achievement and empowers students to be more responsible for their learning (Black & Wiliam, 1998).

Howard Gardner points to the importance of problem and product-related assessments as one of the central features of an educational system:

Standard pencil and paper, short answer tests sample only a small proportion of intellectual abilities and often reward a certain kind of decontextualized facility. The means of assessment we favor should ultimately search for genuine problem-solving or product fashioning skills in individuals across a range of materials. (Gardner, 1993, p. 31)

Assessments that are embedded in science investigations and activities provide evidence of student learning. Evidence of student learning can be seen through:

- data tables, charts, and graphs
- written responses; essays; research reports; reflections; other notebook entries
- verbal explanations; student-student or student-teacher discussion; informal questions
- visuals such as drawings, posters, graphic organizers, and mind maps

- projects and products
- performance tasks and presentations
- teacher-developed criterion-referenced tests

For example, a teacher might use a checklist to record observations of students handling and using equipment correctly and safely during an investigation. A notebook entry might indicate that a student has misinterpreted or misunderstood a concept.

Table 7.1 identifies classroom assessment strategies, defines them, and provides examples of how they might best be used.

Table 7.1   Classroom Assessments and Their Uses

Assessment Strategy	Operational Definitions of Strategies
Observation Checklists	A list of behaviors or tasks that may be assessed through observation. Are students: • Working cooperatively/collaboratively • Practicing safety and carefully handling equipment • Selecting and using equipment wisely • Staying on task; taking responsibility for role or actions • Engaging in meaningful discussion with others • Showing concept understanding • Demonstrating ability to use process skills • Practicing desirable dispositions
Interviews	Teacher to student or student to student conversations; may assess thinking and problem-solving ability. Questions include: • Can you show me an example of . . . ? • Will your data support . . . ? • Did you support your hypothesis? Explain. • How did your group help one another in this project? • What recommendations do you have for more effective learning? • What new questions do you have? • What is the next step for knowing more about this topic?
Notebooks	Carefully designed system for recording information. Entries may include: • Operational questions and hypotheses • Background information, research, and related readings • Action plans for investigations and problem solving • Observations, data, pictures/drawings, scale models • Data tables and graphs; blueprints; charts; illustrations • Graphic organizers • Inferences, conclusions, generalizations, interpretations • Reflections, insights, new questions • Connections to science and other areas of curriculum • Creative writing, stories, poems, and analogies • Information on careers or environmental issues • Notes and information of interest to students

Assessment Strategy	Operational Definitions of Strategies
Products and Projects	Active approaches to learning involving creating something that represents or explains knowledge or applies concepts in a new way. • Products and projects should be designed around important goals and concepts and follow a set of guidelines. • Well-designed projects and products allow students to show their understanding of concepts as well as their thinking and problem-solving abilities. • The presentation or demonstration of a project or product allows teachers to assess communication skills related to speaking and listening. Products or projects may include: • Models, sculpture; collages, diorama • Inventions; audiotapes and videotapes; experiments; interviews; songs • Designs; blueprints; games; stories; news reports; puppet shows • Posters; brochures; pictures; illustrations; totem poles
Assessment Tasks	A set of paper and pencil tasks that require students to apply concepts and skills to a new situation or solve a problem and show their work in detail. Some requirements may be: • Draw or illustrate and label • Create a graph or table • Describe and show a plan • Illustrate and describe an application • Solve a problem with words and pictures
Performance Assessments	Tasks or performances where students show or demonstrate their understandings of concepts and skills. May include: • Active involvement in activities or projects • Applications of concepts to new situations • Show of understanding through products and explanations
Criterion-Referenced Quizzes	Sets of questions: • Often in a multiple choice format that relates directly to the content and context of learning • Three or more items per concept provide the greatest chance for students to show what they know

It is important to establish a rubric for assessments that clearly identifies the indicators of learning that the assessment is targeting. A generic rubric may be designed that can be used with a variety of assessments. It is important to provide frequent and honest feedback (not rewards or punishments) to students regarding their progress in reaching learning goals and standards. Allow opportunities for students to self-assess and use peer review.

Factors such as timeliness, neatness of work, attitude, and the like, although important, should be considered separately from assessments of student learning of instructional goals and standards.

TASKS AND PERFORMANCE ASSESSMENTS

Tasks and performances are similar types of assessments that allow students to apply their knowledge and skills and to provide explanations. Tasks are generally single step activities in a paper/pencil format, while performance assessments are more likely to be multistep activities requiring equipment or materials. Performances may also be formal or informal presentations or demonstrations of learning.

Performance assessments have the same qualities and characteristics that are evident in good instruction—they engage students and challenge them. In addition, performance assessments:

- Assess important goals and standards.
- Are rooted in interesting and meaningful contexts.
- Address multiple indicators of learning by providing opportunities for students to show concept understanding, use of skills, and valued dispositions in a single task.
- Provide opportunities for students to show higher levels of thinking and problem solving.

Table 7.2 provides examples of performance tasks at the primary and intermediate grades; Table 7.3 provides examples at the intermediate and middle grades; Table 7.4 provides examples at the high school levels.

Table 7.2   Performance Tasks for the Primary and Intermediate Grades

Content Area	Performance Tasks
Properties of Objects	• Task 1: Sort the objects on the table into two groups using one property. Write the name of the property you used and tell why you sorted the objects the way you did. • Task 2: Separate the objects using another property. Write the name of the new property. • Task 3: Use the two magnets to demonstrate your understanding of "attract" and "repel."
Characteristics of Organisms	• Task 1: Draw a picture of a pet or other animal. In your picture draw and label at least three things that the animal needs for survival. Explain your drawing. • Task 2: Make a drawing of the part of the human body that is associated with each of the five senses. Next to the structure, write one or more of the types of information we get from each of the senses.

Content Area	Performance Tasks
Life Cycles of Organisms	• Task: Draw and label the stages in the life cycle of a dog or cat (chick, mealworm, cricket, butterfly, or other animal that was studied or is similar to what was studied). Use arrows to show the changes that occur throughout the life cycle. Write a sentence or two to explain the life cycle.
Organisms and Their Environments	• Task: Draw a picture of a park or other natural area. Draw a simple food chain that might be found in the environment. Label each part of the food chain. Be sure to include the source of energy for the food chain. Tell what would happen to the other members if one member of your food chain was no longer available.
Changes in Earth and Sky	• Task 1: Draw a picture of a thermometer, a barometer, a weather vane, and a rain gauge. Next to each picture tell the use for each instrument • Task 2: Demonstrate the use of one or more of the instruments for determining conditions of weather: a thermometer, a barometer, a weather vane, and a rain gauge. • Task 3: Draw the stages of change in the Moon over the course of a month. Label the stages. Be prepared to describe (or write about) why the changes take place.

Table 7.3 Performance Tasks for Intermediate and Middle Grades

Content Area	Performance Tasks
Properties and Changes of Properties in Matter	• Task: Consider the objects on the table. Use the balance and mass set, graduated cylinder, beakers, water, and any other materials in the classroom to find the density of each object. Then, order the objects by density. Draw the objects from the most dense to the least dense.
Transfer of Energy	• Task: Make a drawing to illustrate the principle: Heat moves in predictable ways, flowing from warmer objects to cooler ones, until both reach the same temperature. Label the drawing and explain it.
Structure and Function in Living Systems	• Task 1: Make a poster to show the levels of organization of living things, beginning with cells and ending with ecosystems. Be prepared to describe similarities and differences in the levels. • Task 2: Draw a cell and identify the organelles. Write the function of each organelle next to its name. Draw and identify three different types of cells and tell how they are alike and how they are different. • Task 3: Draw one of the systems of the human body. Label the organs and explain the function of each on the drawing.

Table 7.3 (Continued)

Content Area	Performance Tasks
Reproduction and Heredity	• Task: Make a drawing to show the processes of meiosis and mitosis. Label the stages in the processes. Explain the similarities and differences between the two processes.
Structure of the Earth System	• Task 1: Draw a large boulder and show what will happen to it over time if it is acted upon by forces of weathering and erosion. Include a written description of the forces and the changes that occur. • Task 2: Make a drawing of the water cycle and explain what happens at each of the stages.
Earth in the Solar System	• Task: Draw and label a model of the solar system. Describe the major and minor heavenly bodies and their relationships to one another. Describe the forces that are acting on the solar system.

Table 7.4   Performance Tasks at the High School Level

Content Area	Performance Tasks
Structure of Atoms	• Task: Create a model of an atom that has a minimum of 16 electrons. Be sure to show the components of the nucleus and the electrical charges of the particles that make up the atom.
Structure and Properties of Matter	• Task: Identify a "family of elements" on the Periodic Table and design and give a presentation using visuals to show how the elements in the family are related.
Interactions of Energy and Matter	• Task: Design a demonstration to show that waves—such as sound waves, seismic waves, waves on water, and so forth—have energy and can transfer that energy when they interact with matter.
Molecular Basis of Heredity	• Task 1: Research the history of the discovery of DNA and its structure. Make a timeline to show significant events and the various contributions of scientists. • Task 2: Research some of the ways that DNA is used in forensic science today. Explain how discoveries and research projects led to the use of DNA in forensic science.
The Behavior of Organisms	• Task: Draw the human brain. Identify and label the areas within the brain that are responsible for speech, hearing, and other senses. Explain human behavior in terms of the functioning of nerve cells.
Geochemical Cycles	• Task: Make a poster that shows one way a stable element cycles through the lithosphere, atmosphere, hydrosphere, and living things. Identify and describe the sources of energy involved in the processes.

SUMMATIVE PERFORMANCE ASSESSMENTS

As students work through activities, it is possible to gather evidence of learning of important concepts, skills, and dispositions in many ways. Summative performance assessments may be multistage activities through which a number of concepts, skills, and dispositions can be assessed. The performance will appear to students to be another hands-on activity or set of activities, but it is designed to gather evidence of learning. A summative performance assessment is shown for a unit on States of Matter at the intermediate level.

Activity: Investigating States of Matter

Overview

A performance assessment task has the characteristics of instruction but is used to assess concept understanding and ability to use skills that have been taught through activities, investigations, or experiences. The investigation is used to provide evidence of learning.

Concepts

Materials can exist in different states—solid, liquid, and gas. Some common materials, such as water, can be changed from one state to another by heating or cooling.

A substance has characteristic properties such as density, a boiling point, and others that are independent of the amount of the sample.

Materials and Safety

For each student: a small plastic medicine cup; access to a graduated cylinder that measures 25 mL, tap water, and access to a freezer

Inquiry Question

What happens to water when it changes state?

Engagement

Ask students to describe properties of water and of ice to see what they know. Ask them questions to get them thinking but do not tell them if they are correct or incorrect.

- What changes take place when water changes to ice?
- Does the chemical composition change?
- Does the mass change?
- Does the volume change?

Tell students they are going to investigate what happens to water when it changes state.

Exploration

Directions for Students: You will be investigating the change of state of water from liquid to solid.

- Day 1: You will be given a small cup. Find the mass of the cup and record it on the data table. Using a graduated cylinder, measure 25 mL of water and add this to the cup. Find the new mass and record. Make a mark on the cup to show the level of the water. Put the cup of water into the freezer.

    Predict: How will the cup of water and its mass change when it is put into the freezer overnight?

    I think _____ because:

    _____

- Day 2: Take the cup from the freezer. Find and record the mass of the cup of ice. Complete the following data table.
- Record one or more observations of the cup.

Observations:

1.

2.

3.

Table 7.5   Data Table

1. Mass of cup and water	_____ grams
2. Mass of cup alone	_____ grams
3. Mass of water	_____ grams
4. Mass of cup and ice	_____ grams
5. Mass of cup alone	_____ grams
6. Mass of ice	_____ grams

Write a conclusion related to the inquiry question.

Thought and Discussion

Analysis and Discussion of the Performance Assessment

1. What concepts, skills, and dispositions are assessed in this performance task?

2. What evidence will teachers be able to gather about student learning?

3. What can teachers observe? What types of thinking will students do during this task?

4. Use the analytic scoring rubric shown in Table 7.6 and add a description of what the indicator might look like for each of the three categories. For some indicators, only two categories may be applicable.

Table 7.6   Scoring Rubric for States of Matter

Indicator of Student Learning:	Right On! (2)	Making Progress (1)	Not Yet (0)
Measured mass of cup			
Used graduated cylinder			
Measured mass of cup + water correctly			
Made a prediction			
Measured mass of cup + ice correctly			
Completed the data table			
Recorded observations			
Drew a conclusion			
Answered discussion questions accurately			
Summary showed understanding of concepts			

5. Discuss how rubrics can help students to assess their learning.

Explanation

Answer the questions about your experiment.

1. How did the mass of the cup and the water change when the water changed from liquid to solid? Explain.

2. How is the cup of liquid water similar to and different from the cup of ice?

3. What inference can you make about what happens to water when it changes from a liquid to a solid?

4. Predict: What will happen to the ice if it is left on the table overnight? Explain why you think this will this happen.

5. Predict: What happens to the water if it is left in the cup for a week or more? Why do you think this will happen?

6. Describe what you learned about water when it changes state.

Revisit the Initial Question

How do carefully crafted assessments improve the quality of teaching and enhance student learning?

8

Safe, Supportive, and Challenging Environments for Learning

Indicators of High Quality Teaching

Indicators of High Quality Teaching

High Quality Teaching:

- Utilizes equipment, materials, and resources for enhancing learning and providing a challenging learning environment

Building High Quality Materials to Inform High Quality Instruction

Step Eight:

- Consider resources, equipment, and materials that will be needed for effective instruction.
- Consider management strategies and safety issues.

How do classroom management and safety, equipment, materials, and resources support high quality instruction and enhance student achievement?

CONSIDERATIONS FOR LEARNING ENVIRONMENTS

Similar to having the appropriate weather, accommodations, clothing, and equipment to maximize the enjoyment of a vacation trip, optimum learning environments require appropriate physical settings, attention to safety, a rich assortment of stimulating resources, and professional support. What happens in each classroom depends to a large extent on the knowledge level, beliefs, and abilities of the teacher. However, even best practices may be impaired by physical and operational barriers. Features of an environment that supports learning are:

- Flexible physical setting
- Safety equipment and policies that endorse safety
- Adequate supply of equipment, consumable materials, references, and resources
- Appropriate technology and training in the use of technology
- Abundance of resources that enhance learning
- Funds for consumable materials
- Administrative support and professional development for teachers

The process of creating safe and supportive environments for learning requires planning to ensure that important standards and learning goals are addressed. Most traditional classrooms can be arranged for guided inquiry activities with a few modifications.

Let us not forget the "laboratory for learning" that exists beyond the four walls of the classroom! School sites often provide resources and space around which inquiry investigations can be developed. In addition, informal educational settings throughout the community are rich resources for investigations that introduce or reinforce concepts and extend or apply learning.

Equipment and Supplies

A well-equipped classroom and good classroom management strategies pave the way for a successful program. Basic equipment needed for inquiry-based science will vary with the grade and ability levels of students and the activities that are offered through the science program. Detailed lists of laboratory equipment required for high school level science courses are available from scientific supply companies. At a minimum, the well-equipped science classroom should have:

- Primary balances and informal mass sets such as plastic cubes, bears, or chips in the primary grades; intermediate level balances or scales, formal mass sets, and spring scales for intermediate/middle grades and high school; precision scales or triple beam balances for high school courses
- English/metric tape measures; meter sticks; rulers
- Good quality magnifiers; scissors appropriate for the age level; thermometers for measuring in both °C and °F
- Liter boxes and bottles; plastic graduated cylinders; plastic beakers

- Good quality monocular or binocular microscopes, slides, cover slips, and prepared slides for middle school and high school
- Reference books, trade books, magazines, and audiovisual resources and equipment relevant to the topics and themes studied
- Colorful, informative posters or charts showing concepts or applications of concepts, poster of Periodic Table, posters of skills, and safety posters
- Three-dimensional models of plants, animals, body systems, and geologic features; weather instruments; magnets
- Sample natural materials and specimens such as rocks, minerals, fossils, bug and leaf collections and the like, skulls, owl pellets, animal hides, plants, flowers, and so forth
- An assortment of materials for physical science investigations such as simple machines, cars, kites, gliders, rockets, and other models; small bulbs, batteries, holders, wire, and flashlights for studying electricity; kits for studying robotics
- Chemicals appropriate to investigations; safety equipment needed for working with chemicals
- Computers and software; access to the Internet
- Tape recorders, tape/CD players with appropriate tapes/CDs, cameras, probes, calculators, overhead projectors and transparencies, and other technology that can be used to enhance the teaching/learning process

In addition, students should have access to simple, easily accessible supplies that are needed for investigations such as:

- Aquarium tanks; small containers and boxes; test tubes; several sizes of plastic cups
- Rubber, steel, Styrofoam, and/or plastic balls; ping-pong, golf, and tennis balls
- Consumable materials such as straws, craft sticks, string, tissue paper, poster paper, newsprint, adding machine tape, graph paper, crayons, tape, colored markers, feathers, clay, gravel, sand, soil, aluminum foil, and other materials for use in activities and projects
- An assortment of plants and classroom animals
- An assortment of small objects, maps, globes, and other materials related to activities and investigations

Consumable materials will vary with the topics and activities that are selected to meet the educational goals for a specific grade level. But some commonly used materials are: rubber bands, string, clay, paper towels, wax paper, construction paper, paper plates and cups, Styrofoam cups, sugar, salt, sand, soil, graph paper, newspaper, and/or rolls of paper or newsprint.

Teachers can offer more creative instruction when the materials and resources they need are readily available. Materials should reside in the classroom where they will be used and stored in cabinets or stackable boxes for easy access. Donations of materials are often sought from parents and/or parent-teacher organizations. Grants from local or state agencies or organizations might be available to start programs or to support ongoing programs in the elementary or middle grades where budgets are tight. School systems that value science education will have significant budgets for science equipment and consumable materials at all grade levels.

Integrating Mathematics and Science

Note that laboratory materials for effective science at all levels include equipment used for mathematics education. Investigations leading to the understanding of science concepts often require students to collect and record both qualitative observations and quantitative data. What better way to teach concepts of mass, volume, and temperature, linear measurement, geometry, probability and statistics, and graphing than through the context of science!

Science education builds an understanding of mathematics that is rooted in concepts and principles of the physical world with real-world applications. Measurement, using numbers, and recording data are important process skills of science that overlap with mathematics. In addition, both mathematics and science value analytical and critical reasoning and problem-solving skills.

Physical Environment

Classrooms should be stimulating environments! Pictures, posters, and artwork add color and interest. Models, mobiles, projects, and student work samples add to the appearance of the classroom as a "laboratory for learning." Posters showing process and thinking skills and important topic-related vocabulary words are reminders to teachers and students to use the vocabulary of science in their conversations and explanations.

There is no set arrangement for an inquiry-based science classroom, but some factors that add to an exciting climate and promote cooperative group work, hands-on learning, and independent study include:

- Properly ventilated classrooms, store rooms, and workrooms
- Flat desks or tables that allow two to four students to work together
- Sinks and the availability of water
- Well-equipped laboratory stations for middle school and high school
- Separate tables or shelves for equipment, books, and other resources
- An area for students to work on projects individually or collaboratively
- Centers for relearning or extended learning
- Computers, software, and Internet access; areas for use of technology, such as video equipment and microscopes
- Tables or shelves for displaying products, mobiles, and models; wall space to display posters/drawings, time lines, two-dimensional models
- Posters of process skills words to remind teachers and students to use the vocabulary of science as they describe investigations
- Posters or word walls with key vocabulary words for a particular unit to prompt students to use the words in writing and speaking and to reinforce spelling

CLASSROOM SAFETY

Safety should be the first consideration in the school and classroom. Rules of safety must be followed at **all** times. Federal and state agencies offer guidelines for safety in schools. Schools should have safety plans for each grade level span (K–5, 6–8, and 9–12) that identify such things as:

- Safe standard operating procedures
- First aid and emergency equipment and use
- Safe laboratory practices
- Guidelines for keeping animals in the classroom
- Safe housekeeping practices
- Chemical procurement, storage, and distribution
- Guidelines for waste disposal
- Biological hazards
- Electrical safety
- Other relative safety information

Signs should be posted and lighted as required, and fire and disaster drills should be conducted regularly. Students need to be aware of emergency telephone numbers and exits, evacuation routes and proper response behaviors, and safety equipment, such as first aid kits, eye wash stations, fire extinguishers, and fire blankets, as well as procedures for the safe and efficient use of equipment and materials.

A safe and effective science laboratory experience requires responsible conduct on the part of students, cleanliness, and lack of clutter. Students should not eat or drink or put anything into their mouths in a lab and appropriate safety goggles should be used whenever there is a threat to eyes from projectiles or chemical splashes.

Safety equipment at all levels will vary somewhat with the types of activities offered. In addition to the guidelines specified on the safety plan, common sense and an atmosphere of mutual respect and consideration for others are required.

Students should understand and adhere to safe practices at all times. They and their parents or guardians should sign a "safety contract" indicating their understanding of expected student behaviors.

Specific guidelines for each grade level span are beyond the scope of this book. A list of excellent Web sites and resources is provided. State departments of education generally provide specific guidelines for safety plans and resources and make these available to the school systems within their states.

RESOURCES

Mercier, Paul (1996). *Laboratory safety pocket handbook.* Amsterdam, NY: Genium Publishing Corporation.

Safety in Academic Chemistry Laboratories. Available from: American Chemical Society, 1155 16th St. NW, Washington, DC 20003

Manual of Safety and Health Hazards in the School Science Laboratory.

Safety in the School Science Laboratory.

Clair Woods. *Safety in Science Laboratories.*

> The preceding three titles are available from: Laboratory Safety Workshop, 101 Oak St., Wellesley, MA 02181–4723

Prudent Practices for Handling Chemicals in Laboratories and Prudent Practices for Disposal of Chemicals in Laboratories. Available from: National Academy Press, 2101 Constitution Avenue, Washington, DC 20418

Steere, N. (ed.). *Handbook of Laboratory Safety*, 4th ed. Available from: CRC Press, 2000 Corporate Blvd. NW, Boca Raton, FL 33431

INTERNET RESOURCES

Occupational Safety and Health Administration

OSHA Laboratory Standard–29 CFR 1910.1450: http://www.osha.gov/

OSHA's mission is to ensure the safety and health of U.S. workers by setting and enforcing standards; providing training, outreach, and education; establishing partnerships; and encouraging continual improvement in workplace safety and health.

The Laboratory Safety Institute: http://www.labsafety.org

The Laboratory Safety Institute is a nonprofit, international educational organization for health, safety, and environmental affairs. They offer courses, workshops, and materials to enable teachers and students to learn to care about their health and safety, learn to identify life's hazards and how to protect themselves, and create a safer and healthier learning and working environment.

National Science Teachers Association Position Statement: http://www.nsta.org/positionstatement&psid-32

The site includes the position statement and a list of resources.

Flinn Scientific's Middle School Science Safety Contract: http://www.flinnsci.com/Documents/miscPDFs/safety_contract_MS.pdf

The middle school safety contract identifies 21 safety rules for middle school students. The agreement must be signed by both the students and the parent or guardian before the child is allowed to participate in science activities.

Montgomery County Public Schools Science Safety: http://www.mcps.k12.md.us/curriculum/science/instr/safety.htm#Anchor-Safety-49575

This site offers a wealth of information and resources related to science safety including:

Complete Science Safety Manual

Science Safety and the Law

Safety videos

Safety review, safety test, and safety contract

Flinn Scientific Science Teacher Resources: http://www.flinnsci.com/ Sections/Safety/safety.asp

Flinn Scientific offers resources and Web sites related to science safety.

Project Six Resource Page: Laboratory Safety: http://www.facstaff .bucknell.edu/nyquist/bi317/resources/project6_safe_res.html

This site offers an extensive list of Web sites and articles on safety in the biology laboratory and field. The topics include:

Resources on the Internet

Articles dealing with administrative and legal issues

Hands-on science safety

Electrical safety

Safety with biological organisms

Safety with chemicals

Secondary Science Education: Northern Illinois University: http:// niuhep.physics.niu.edu/~scienceed/p495/safety.htm

The site offers links to information and articles related to classroom safety. In addition, a number of Web sites related to safety in the science classroom are offered including:

Safety in the professional and educational setting

Online safety course

Maryland and Texas science safety guidelines

High school chemistry lab safety

Sample high school science lab safety rules

Elementary school science safety

OSHA

American Chemical Society Safety Committee

National Fire Protection Association Codes and Standards

Contact lens safety in the science classroom

CLASSROOM MANAGEMENT

The teacher is the architect who designs the micro-world of the classroom. The values, attitudes, and social skills the teacher models set the tone for the class.

Kay Burke

Students generally enjoy working in a laboratory or field setting since these learning environments resemble those of a scientist or researcher. A well-managed classroom, laboratory, or field experience, with the teacher functioning as a facilitator, is necessary for maximum learning to occur. A classroom climate founded on responsibility, respect, and a desire to learn is critical. Since working safely with science equipment in a laboratory setting requires students to operate within a boundary of appropriate behaviors, students should help to determine rules and safe operating procedures for labs. Students should also help to determine consequences of inappropriate behavior. Their input will help them to remember the rules and proper procedures.

Consideration should be given to grouping patterns, procedures for obtaining and returning equipment, methods of dispensing materials and specimens, safety when working with materials, and procedures for disposing of trash and cleaning the work space. Rules for lab and safety precautions should be displayed on posters as reminders to students.

Positive teacher-student interactions are important in establishing a climate of cooperation and respect. Kay Burke (2001) advises teachers to offer professional responses to inappropriate student behaviors or comments and to model the rule of "respect the dignity of others." She offers both a list of teacher behaviors that may create behavior problems and a list of approaches for proactive teachers to prevent behavior problems. Some of the proactive approaches are:

- Anticipate potential behavior problems by assigning potential problem students to different groups, provide both verbal and written directions to eliminate confusion and frustration, engage in private conversations with students to determine problems, make allowances for students with disabilities, encourage peer tutoring, and elicit the support of counselors to get suggestions for meeting the needs of students.
- Diffuse minor problems before they become major disturbances.
- Address disruptive behaviors immediately and address them quickly, calmly, and confidently; remove offender from the group or class and provide alternatives for learning.
- Follow up with private conversations to determine problems and to suggest positive approaches to dealing with problems.

The key to successful classroom management is prevention—and prevention should begin the first minute of the first day of class.

(Burke, 2001, pp. 35–37)

Management Strategies for Inquiry-Based Science

Give and Take Technique. Students who have not had experience working responsibly in a laboratory or small group setting should not be set free to carry out complex science investigations. In the beginning, investigations can be broken down into a series of smaller tasks. Following discussion of directions and expectations, students can work on a single task and engage in a group discussion of that task before working on the next one. Students are less likely to make mistakes or to get off task if they have only a single task to perform in a given amount of time. This "give and take" technique, with the teacher facilitating and interacting with students, allows students to practice appropriate behaviors and build an understanding of expected lab behavior in a safe and positive way.

Cooperative Learning. Cooperative learning strategies allow students to assume a variety of roles, practice responsible behaviors, and develop valued dispositions with more freedom and flexibility. Students may be assigned a specific role by teachers or through a random selection process. Strategies should be introduced slowly, providing multiple opportunities for students to practice patience and persistence while learning to work cooperatively and collaboratively with peers.

While working in cooperative groups, students should show respect for others and be accountable for their part of the learning experience. Care should be taken to ensure that each student has a role or responsibility and that each student is making a contribution. Grouping patterns and roles for students should be changed periodically to allow for varied responsibilities and social interactions between students of all ability and interest levels. It is important that students, working individually or in groups, understand directions and have the appropriate materials and equipment.

Before long, students will be able to assume responsibility for working on multiple tasks and for making decisions about the use of time, resources, and equipment. Alternative arrangements can be made for students who do not accept the invitation to work in a lab or group setting. Individual contracts can be made with students and alternative resources, such as computers, books, videotapes, models, or instructional games might be available for their use.

Role of Teacher. In a well-managed classroom, teachers are able to act as facilitators of learning and are better able to interact with students to guide learning, ask probing questions, and conduct informal assessments of learning. By working through purposeful activities in a learner-centered environment, students are more likely to:

- Make careful observations
- Develop important concepts
- Develop skills and valued dispositions
- Take careful measurements
- Collect, record, and analyze data
- Solve problems with patience and persistence
- Develop and apply analytical reasoning
- Develop critical and creative thinking skills
- Develop speaking and listening skills
- Take ownership for their work

┌───┐

Thought and Discussion

Case Study of Classroom Management

Read the case study. Discuss what advice you would offer Ms. Rogers for conducting this lab again.

Case Study

Ms. Rogers, a middle school science teacher, was planning to conduct a lab activity with students who did not have much laboratory experience. She had six tables with four students at each table, and each group was given one lab investigation with directions and one data sheet. The teacher briefly introduced the activity by telling the students what they were going to do in the activity. She instructed them to read the directions while she passed out the materials. She reminded students that talking was not allowed.

Ms. Rogers had all her equipment on a cart. As she began distributing the materials, students began talking quietly among themselves. Ms. Rogers reprimanded them for talking, telling them to be quiet and to read the directions. As students got their materials, they stared at one another, waiting to be told what to do or for someone in the group to act as leader.

After a few minutes, one student approached Ms. Rogers and reluctantly pointed out that her group did not think they had the appropriate materials to conduct the investigation.

Ms. Rogers gave an angry sigh, appeared confused, and told the students they would not do the lab that day. Without saying another word, she collected the materials and directed the students to read the chapter in the textbook for the remainder of the class period.

└───┘

MANAGEMENT IN INFORMAL SETTINGS

Visits to informal science centers should be well planned with expectations for student conduct and learning communicated to students well in advance. Students should be well aware of the purpose of the experience and help to plan the experience. They should approach the visit with a heightened curiosity and sense of wonderment. Students should have responsibilities for taking notes or pictures, making observations, collecting and recording data, interviewing, drawing, or gathering information at the site. Sites may provide materials that guide students to educational displays and provide valuable information. Many sites offer suggestions for activities to prepare students to get the maximum benefit from their visit.

Programs at informal science centers often focus on topics that align with curricular goals. For example, the Bronx Zoo Education Department and Wildlife Conservation Society offers a program featuring diversity of lifestyles. The program uses the zoo as a laboratory through which students discover animal adaptations firsthand.

North Carolina State University's Science House offers hands-on science and mathematics programs that emphasize the contributions of scientists and inventors of all cultures. The goal of the program is to promote interest in careers in science and mathematics, especially in students from underrepresented groups. Both of these enrichment programs address important aspects of the middle school science curriculum. Descriptions of these and other science, mathematics, and engineering enrichment programs for precollege students and teachers nationwide can be found through the Science Training Programs Directory for Teachers and Students (STP). The Web site is www .sciserv.org/stp.

In some environments, students will be a captive audience, such as when observing a film, demonstration, or program. Groups of students may be guided through buildings or grounds by staff that point out noteworthy objects or interesting events of the present or past and provide valuable information along the way. Bus or boat tours of historic sites and walking tours of homes, castles, churches, and parks are examples.

In museums, zoological parks, amusement parks, and the like, students and their supervisors may be left on their own to explore the exhibits, make observations, and engage in activities. In this case, it is important that the supervising adults are well aware of the learning goals for the experience, have a good rapport with the students, and are able to direct student attention to exhibits and activities that meet the instructional goals. In all cases, teacher-student ratios should be small to ensure safety, attend to student needs, facilitate student involvement in activities, and maximize learning.

Thought and Discussion

1. Create a management plan for a visit to an informal science center. Consider things that can be done before, during, and after the visit to ensure a safe and productive experience. Use Table 8.1 as a guide for planning.

2. Select a setting that is familiar to you or one that you have visited. Use the Instructional Planning Guide for a Field Experience in Table 8.2 to map out details for the instructional experience.

   a. Identify one or more key concepts that may be explored and learned through a visit to the site.

   b. Describe possible learning experiences and activities that might be done at the site.

   c. Identify materials and resources or prior learning experience that would enhance the learning experiences.

   d. Identify ways to follow up and process the experience to reinforce learning. Share your plans.

Table 8.1   Planning Guide for an Out-of-Classroom Learning Experience

Things to Do Before the Trip	Things to Do at the Site	Follow-Up Activities Experience

Table 8.2   Instructional Planning Guide for a Field Experience

Setting: _____

Points to Consider	Before	During	After
Key Concepts or Focus of Learning			
Learning Experiences or Activities			
Materials and Resources			
Ways to Reinforce Learning			

CREATIVE CLASSROOMS

How exciting for students to come to school one day and enter their science classroom as though they were walking through a cell membrane and into a cell! This creative classroom surrounded students with models of organelles and other cell features for the time they were studying the unit on cell theory.

Rain forest environments may be constructed to immerse students in the colorful and complex variety of living and nonliving things about which they will learn. For example, the large leaves of rain forest plants provide an opportunity for students to make comparisons to plant leaves found in other ecosystems. The unusual animals and plants fascinate inquiry questions for further investigation.

Models of the atomic structures of various elements displayed throughout the classroom provide concrete images of abstract concepts for middle school and high school students. In a study of force and motion, posters and working models of Rube Goldberg-type "contraptions" not only attract attention, but also allow students to trace the problem-solving schemes and study the functions of the simple machines used to create the schemes.

Classrooms can be set up with workstations offering different activities or sets of activities, enabling students to select some or all of the activities as needed. Centers may be created to provide audiovisual equipment and materials, books, and other reading materials; hands-on activities and equipment; games and puzzles; and materials for relearning or extended learning. Creative classrooms invite participation and motivate students to get more involved in learning.

Revisit the Initial Question

How do classroom management and safety, equipment, materials, and resources support high quality instruction and enhance student achievement?

9

Eight Steps to High Quality Instruction and Student Achievement

High quality instruction begins with high quality curriculum materials. Carefully crafted science units and lessons, rich with opportunities for students to develop concepts and skills, provide a guiding framework for delivering high quality instruction. Such materials focus on important concepts and skills and describe effective practices that accommodate learners and promote student achievement.

Many commercial and teacher-developed products include components of high quality. The eight indicators of high quality described in this book provide a set of criteria against which to assess instructional materials. When teachers use the criteria to analyze and modify existing units, they develop a greater awareness of:

- the alignment of standards with instruction and assessment
- the content, skills, and dispositions of science
- the interdisciplinary nature of science
- equipment, materials, and resources to enhance learning
- creative ways to engage students in learning concepts and skills

- strategies for differentiating instruction and accommodating learning styles
- strategies for ongoing assessment to inform students and monitor and guide instruction

The process invites teachers to add creative ideas, vary instructional approaches, and enrich activities and experiences through which students will learn.

Two examples of the application of the eight step model are provided in this chapter: Applying the Eight Steps to a Unit on Plants and Applying the Eight Steps to a Unit on Rocks and Minerals. These sections offer specific examples for thought and discussion that enable administrators, teacher leaders, and teachers to further clarify and frame their understanding of high quality curriculum and instruction.

EXAMPLE 1: APPLYING THE EIGHT STEPS TO A UNIT ON PLANTS

Unit development is a process that allows the developer to add creative ideas, approaches, and strategies to an instructional plan. One teacher unit may not serve the needs of another teacher, but thoughtfully crafted instructional units provide good examples of varied ways to accommodate the needs and interests of learners.

The eight step model is shown with descriptions and examples from a unit on plants that was designed for fifth grade students who had no prior laboratory experience with the topic.

The activities that were selected for the unit address intermediate level standards and concepts related to the structure and function of plants and build in complexity as they introduce the use of the microscope and investigate cell structure, seeds and plant reproduction, and the importance of plants.

The application of the eight steps to the unit offers an example of one teacher's approach to instruction and assessment. For some of the steps, examples from the plant unit are shown; for other steps, detailed descriptions are given along with ideas and suggestions for exploring concepts and assessing student learning.

> **Step One: Select a topic or theme from the state or local framework for science education for your grade level. Research and review content information about this topic.**

Content Standards

- Structure and Function in Living Systems
  - Living systems at all levels of organization demonstrate the complementary nature of structure and function.
  - Important levels of organization for structure and function include cells, organs, tissues, organ systems, whole organisms, and ecosystems.
  - Cells carry on the many functions needed to sustain life.

- Reproduction and Heredity
  - Reproduction is a characteristic of all living systems; because no individual organism lives forever, reproduction is essential to the continuation of every species.
  - Plants reproduce sexually—the egg and sperm are produced in the flowers of flowering plants.

Background Information for Teachers

A review of current standards-related content from reliable sources, including books, Web sites, professionals, videotapes, and other resources, will highlight important concepts and give teachers information and ideas for activities and experiences. Many of the resources identified by teachers may be useful to students who want to extend their learning through projects or research.

> **Step Two: Select a set of key concepts and principles appropriate for the grade level around which the unit will be developed. Design one or more graphic organizers to show relationships between concepts or concept categories for the unit.**

> **Step Three: Consider process skills of science, critical thinking skills, and dispositions to include or emphasize in the unit.**

Basic concepts were selected for the plant unit that address plant structure and function, seed structure and plant reproduction, cell structure and function, introduction to and use of microscopes, the importance of plants in nature, and the value of plants to society.

Key Concepts

- The four main parts of plants are the stem, leaves, root, and flowers, and each part has a specific structure and function that serves the plant and allows the plant to live, grow, and reproduce. Flowering plants produce seeds. Seeds are not all alike. Seeds are one way that plants reproduce.
- Leaves can be classified in a variety of ways using properties such as venation, shape, size, and type. Dichotomous keys are used to classify objects. Properties of leaves can be observed using a magnifier.
- The age of trees or branches can be determined by studying their cross sections. For each year of growth, the tree grows an additional layer of cells, which adds an annual ring.
- Plant cells can be observed firsthand by using a microscope. Plant cells have a nucleus, chloroplasts, a cell wall, cytoplasm, and a cell membrane. Animal cells do not have cell walls or chloroplasts.
- The transfer of energy in an ecosystem begins with green plants (producers). Chlorophyll enables plants to make their own food. Humans rely on plants for food and other nonfood related products.

Graphic Organizers

Teachers may wish to design one graphic organizer that links all of the concepts in the unit, or they may wish to develop graphic organizers for each concept, similar to those students might design. The basic frameworks for graphic organizers described and shown in Chapter 6 should be used by students to create mental models and make sense of concepts.

The Venn diagram and the dichotomous key are two examples of organizers used in activities. Four graphic organizers for the concepts in this unit are shown in Figures 9.1, 9.2, 9.3, and 9.4.

Figure 9.1   Functions of Plant Parts

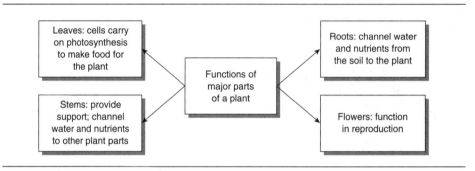

Figure 9.2   Types of Leaves

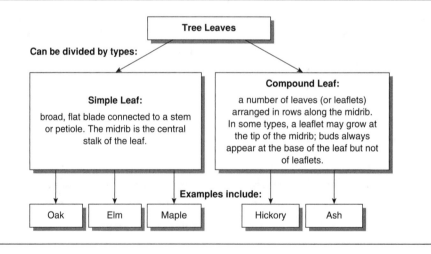

Figure 9.3   The Life Cycle of a Plant

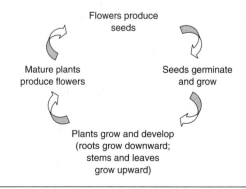

Figure 9.4   Similarities and Differences of Seed Types

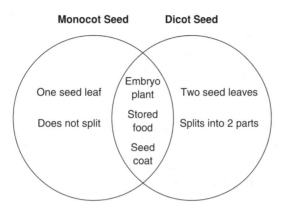

Process and Thinking Skills

Important process and thinking skills emphasized in the inquiry-based unit include observation, classification, inference, measurement, prediction, collecting and recording data, drawing conclusions, making comparisons, critical and creative thinking, accessing and using information, reasoning and problem solving, applying knowledge, and making connections.

Dispositions

The dispositions and expectations that are emphasized in this unit are:

- Ability to work in cooperative groups
- Ability to act safely and responsibly
- Ability to understand and do scientific inquiry
- Ability to show honesty and respect

Step Four: Create a context for meaningful learning.

In the process of creating a meaningful context, it is important to consider a variety of ways to make learning meaningful and enjoyable for students. A context for learning should be:

- Interesting
- Relevant
- Purposeful
- Challenging

For a unit on plants, students might be invited to assist a botanist with research or be a part of a project at a community park or nursery. The unit may begin with a field experience or a presentation by a scientist or other professional, or it may relate to a state or community problem or issue.

Experiences bring out questions around which instruction may be developed. In our unit, students were invited to participate in conducting research on plants. They eagerly accepted the invitation, which required their willingness to work cooperatively and to act responsibly.

Students were taken outdoors to observe and study different types of plants and draw them. Indoors, the traditional classroom was rearranged to resemble a science laboratory. Desks were clustered to form small stations. Instructions for investigations, equipment, and materials were set at each station. Students had access to some of the materials, such as slides and plant material, from a central, teacher-monitored station.

Following their work at each station, students cleaned the equipment and tables and left the station ready for the next scientist(s). Small groups of students or individual students rotated among the stations throughout the week and recorded their work in notebooks.

Step Five: Research learning activities and experiences. Consider those that are readily available; determine activities to be developed or modified. Use a consistent format for crafting each instructional activity and experience.

- **Include multiple and varied methods and strategies for meeting the needs of learners.**
- **Consider activities and experiences for relearning and for extended learning.**

Careful consideration should be given to the selection of activities that will provide the most powerful learning experiences for students. Refer to a variety of instructional resources for activities. Activities can be modified to accommodate needs or interests. A format such as the Five E's provides consistency and clarity to activities and experiences. The carefully designed plan provides a script for the delivery of high quality instruction. Whenever possible, design activities and experiences that offer novelty, variety, and choice.

Novelty

Children enjoy new and novel approaches to learning. They enjoy acting like scientists. They feel important and take pride in their work when learning is meaningful and enjoyable.

Variety and Choice

Offering a variety of activities and experiences not only accommodates learning styles and multiple intelligences, but also enables students to experience different ways of learning. Whenever possible, students should be given a choice of learning activities. Their selections may increase motivation and result in more meaningful learning.

Crafting Activities and Experiences

A variety of approaches should be used to address important concepts and skills. Some approaches are listed here.

Laboratory Activities

Laboratory investigations and active learning experiences should be developed around important concepts using teacher- or student-generated inquiry questions. Students may work on the same activities at the same time with more teacher direction, or stations can be set up that allow students to work in small groups or individually on different activities with teachers acting as facilitators. Additional laboratory and active learning experiences may be offered to students as alternative pathways, relearning, or extending learning.

Table 9.1 shows concepts, inquiry questions, and laboratory activities and active learning experiences for the unit on plants.

Table 9.1   Concept-Related Inquiry Questions and Activities

Concept	Inquiry Questions	Activities
Four main parts of plants are the stem, leaves, root, and flowers. Each part has a specific structure and function that serves the plant and allows the plant to live, grow, and reproduce. Seeds are not all alike.	• What are the parts of a plant? How does each part function in the plant? • How does each part of a flower function in reproduction? • How are monocot seeds similar to and different from dicot seeds?	• Use magnifiers to observe roots, stems, leaves, and flowers. • Use a microscope to observe prepared slides of plants. • Make slides of plant parts; observe, draw, and label them. • Dissect a flower. • Draw and label the parts of the flower; write the function for each flower part. • Dissect monocot and dicot seeds; identify features such as the seed leaves, stored food, seed coat, and embryo plant. • Identify similarities and differences.
Leaves can be classified in a variety of ways using properties such as venation, shape, size, type, description, and so forth. Dichotomous keys are based on properties. Properties of leaves can be observed using a magnifier.	• What are properties of leaves that can be used to classify them? • How can leaves be classified according to properties?	• Observe the structures of leaves using a magnifier. Identify similarities and differences in leaves. • Separate leaves into categories that do and do not have specific properties. • Create a dichotomous key for classifying the leaves.

(Continued)

Table 9.1 (Continued)

Concept	Inquiry Questions	Activities
The age of trees or branches can be determined by studying the cross sections. For each year of growth, the tree grows an additional layer of cells, which adds an annual ring.	• How do we tell the age of a tree? • What is the function of bark on a tree?	• Observe "tree cookies"; count annual rings to determine the ages. • Measure the various sizes of growth rings in millimeters. • Infer why rings may be of different widths. Research reasons. • Infer the function of bark on a tree or branch. Support your inference.
Plant cells can be observed by using a microscope. Plant cells have a nucleus, chloroplasts, a cell wall, cytoplasm, and a cell membrane. Animal cells do not have cell walls or chloroplasts.	• What can we learn about cells by observing them under a microscope? • How do plant cells differ from animal cells?	• Use microscopes to observe plant and animal cells. Draw and label major cell parts. • Research the functions of major cell parts. • Identify similarities and differences between plant and animal cells. • Use a Venn diagram to show similarities and differences.
Plants are useful to humans for food and other nonfood related products. Plants are the basis of the food chain.	• Where are examples of plants and/or plant material in our homes? How do we use plants? • What parts of plants are most commonly used as food? • What are some other uses for plants besides food, such as sources for drugs, medicine, fiber for fabrics, and so forth?	• Make a list of items found in your home and identify what plant they came from and what part of the plant they came from. For example, the dining room table is made of wood; the wood came from the trunk of a tree. • Take a survey in the class to determine which plant parts are eaten the most; collect and graph data. • Research other uses for plants. Find examples that relate to the lives of students and needs, interests, and problems or issues in the community, state, or nation.
Extensions: Careers; Connections to Technology and Society; Plants in History, Music, Art, and Literature.	• What are some occupations that work with plants? • How can we apply what we learned about plants to other areas of the curriculum?	• Research careers in which one works either directly or indirectly with plants. • Some career areas are florist, forester, carpenter, pharmacist, naturalist, landscape architect, landscaper, or farmer. • Research evidence of the importance of plants or plants as the main subject in history, literature, art, and music.

Projects and Products

As students work through their units, they ask new questions that might be answered through simple experiments or research projects. For example, in the plant unit, some students tested the effects of light, heat, and water on plant growth. Other students wrote and illustrated stories about plants to share with younger students. These projects and others designed by students provided opportunities to reinforce and extend learning.

Outdoor Activities

Using the outdoors and informal learning centers can enhance concept awareness and create wonder. Some examples are:

- Take trips to the school grounds and nearby parks to observe and investigate plants in their natural environments.
- Visit a nature center, garden center, plant nursery, or botanic gardens.
- Study various ways that plants adapt to their environments.
- Collect fallen leaves from the natural environment and observe, sort, and classify them.

Activities for Relearning

Classroom centers or stations can be set up for relearning and extended learning. Sets of materials should be available for students to use in after school programs or to take home. In addition, books, videotapes, and other resources should be available for direct instruction. Struggling students might be provided with student or adult tutors.

Opportunities for Extended Learning

Opportunities should be available for students to extend their learning through books and videotapes, access to the Internet, additional activities, experiments, projects, and experiences beyond the classroom.

Connections to Other Subject Areas

Units should be integrated with other areas of the curriculum such as language arts, art, photography, music, health and nutrition, economics, geography, history, and mathematics whenever possible. Through an integrated approach to learning, students become aware of the interdisciplinary nature of science and the interconnectedness of knowledge.

Reading, writing, and critical thinking are basic components of science instruction. Table 9.2 offers suggestions for integrating reading, writing, and critical thinking with the unit on plants.

Table 9.2   Suggestions for Integrating Reading, Writing, and Thinking

Suggestions for Reading	Suggestions for Writing	Suggestions for Critical and Creative Thinking
• Topic-specific trade books and reference books for reading and research. • Read poems and stories related to topic. Summarize important ideas. • Create a word wall of terms and vocabulary from the readings. • Use terms and vocabulary of science in discussion.	• Design and use a science notebook. • Writing prompts for students: Write a letter to a plant telling it how much you appreciate all that it does for you. Be sure to include information you learned about plants. Use the correct form for letter writing. Write a poem about a plant. The poem should be 16 lines long, or create two writings of 8 lines each. The poem should use appropriate vocabulary and show what you know about plants.	• Create graphic organizers to show relationships between concepts. • Create analogies to show relationships between plant parts and relationships of plants to other things. • Design an investigation to solve a problem or answer a new question. • Create data tables and graphs to use in the investigation. • Carry out the investigation and record procedures and data. • Analyze data. • Communicate results.

> **Step Six: Include a variety of ways for students to frame thought, link new learning to prior learning, and make connections to their lives, technology, and society.**
>
> • Sequence activities and experiences.
> • Build concept understanding from basic to more complex.
> • Develop a student notebook that reflects what students will design, do, record, write, research, and so forth throughout the unit.

Sequencing

Sequencing activities from basic to more complex learning builds concept understanding while allowing students to relearn or extend learning as needed. Each activity in the developmental sequence should include questions that enable students to reflect on processes and link new learning to prior learning. Questions should prompt students to apply concepts to their lives, technology, and society in order to establish relevance and enhance meaning.

Using Notebooks

Using science notebooks is an excellent way to integrate reading and writing with science. Once the activities are selected and sequenced, a notebook can be designed for use throughout the unit. The notebook can be used to focus attention on important concepts and facilitate learning. In addition, the notebook provides evidence of student learning. A science notebook might include any or all of these components:

- Inquiry questions or problems of interest
- Predictions and hypotheses
- Action plans and background information
- Observations and data
- Student-generated data tables, graphs, drawings, and graphic organizers
- Conclusions, summaries, and reflections of learning
- Connections to technology and society
- Information on careers, applications of concepts, and research
- New questions

Connections to Technology and Society

There are many applications of plants to technology and society. Plants and plant products are very much a part of "everyday life." Research questions can be designed to focus on the importance of plants. In addition, research questions can be designed to help students to recognize the geographic and economic significance of plants. Some examples are:

- How have plants helped to shape the economy of various parts of the country? Consider the importance of forests, vineyards, corn and wheat fields, grasslands, orchards, greenhouses, and so forth to the areas in which they are located and to the country as a whole.
- What plants are native to the part of the country where you live? What plants have been brought into the country from other countries? For what purpose(s) were they brought? Are those plants helpful or harmful? What is the difference between a native plant and a weed? Are weeds helpful or harmful? How are weeds controlled?
- How are plants useful for combating infection and disease?
- Why are rain forests being destroyed? What may be the long-range effects of rain forest destruction?

> **Step Seven: Design a rich assortment of formative assessments.**
>
> - **Establish rubrics to enable students to self-assess.**
> - **Use assessment data to assess effectiveness of unit.**

Multiple and varied assessments used throughout the instructional process serve as diagnostic tools to provide evidence of student learning. Table 9.3

Table 9.3 Assessments for Learning

Source of Evidence	Evidence of Learning
Data sheets for activities and experiments	• Data tables and graphs • Responses to reflection questions
Notebook entries	• Inquiry questions and action plans • Drawings and illustrations • Data tables and graphs • Conclusions based on data • Answers to reflective questions • Summaries of learning • Connections to technology and society • Researched information • Extended learning
Observation checklists	• Participation in discussion • Working in cooperative group • Following safety rules • Staying "on task" • Showing respect for equipment
Products	• Models, mobiles, and inventions • Posters, brochures, and maps • Drawings and diagrams • Power Point programs • Lab reports and essays • Portfolios
Performances	• Presentations of projects and products • Explanations of data • Demonstrations • Performance tasks • Interviews • Defend a position and debate
Teacher-made quizzes and tests	• Teacher-developed questions • Open-ended writing prompts • Performance tasks

shows a number of assessments that can be used for a unit on plants. Rubrics should be designed to communicate learning goals and expectations to students. Students can use rubrics for self-assessment.

Sample Performance Assessment for the Unit on Plants

This paper/pencil task was used to assess some of the objectives of the plant unit. Other evidence of learning included journal entries, projects, observations and explanations, and teacher-student interviews.

A rubric was provided for self-assessment. Following this assessment task, students were given opportunities for relearning and extended learning.

What I Know About Plants

Part I: Draw a flowering plant. Include and label four important parts.

Tell the function of each part:
(a) stem
(b) leaves
(c) roots
(d) flowers

Part II: Classify the leaves shown in the drawings below. Identify one property you will use to sort the leaves into two categories. Write the name of the property and put the letter of each leaf into the boxes that show whether the leaves have or do not have the property.

Note to teacher: Add drawings of leaves A and B parallel venation, C, D, and E palmate venation.

Table 9.4   Data Table for Classification

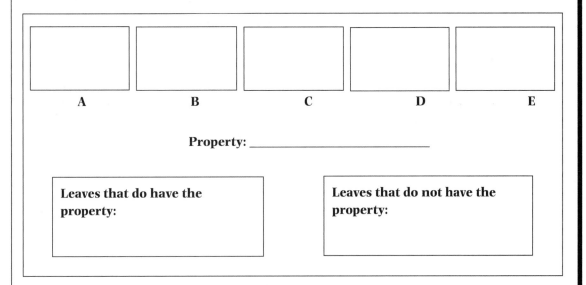

Property: _____

Leaves that do have the property:	Leaves that do not have the property:

Part III: How do tree rings indicate the age of a tree? How does a tree create rings?

Part IV: List three ways that plants are useful to humans (other than as food).
(1)
(2)
(3)

Part V: List three common foods that are plants and tell what part of a plant each one is.

Table 9.5   Data Table

Food	Plant Part
(1)	(1)
(2)	(2)
(3)	(3)

Part VI: Complete the Venn diagram. Identify at least two ways that plant and animal cells are structurally alike. List two ways they are structurally different. Figure 9.5 includes possible answers.

Figure 9.5   Comparing Plant and Animal Cells

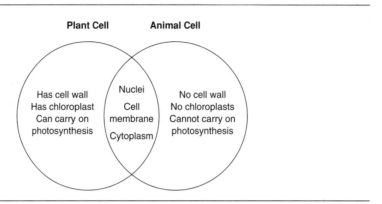

Part VII: Describe how using a microscope helps you to understand plants better.

Rubric for Plant Unit Assessment

The rubric developed for the performance task is an analytic scoring rubric. Each indicator of learning is given a score. (Note: Indicators of learning that are considered to be more important can be weighted, such as X 2.)

The student:

Part I:
- Drew a plant showing leaves, stem, roots, and flowers   1   0
- Labeled each of the four parts correctly   4   3   2   1   0
- Wrote the function of each part   4   3   2   1   0

Part II:
- Identified a property   1   0
- Classified each of the five leaves into 2 categories   2   1   0

Part III:
- Explained tree rings   2   1   0

Part IV:
- Listed three ways plants are useful   3   2   1   0

Part V:
- Listed three common foods and their parts   3   2   1   0

Part VI:
- Listed two ways plant and animal cells are alike   2   1   0
- Listed two ways plant and animal cells are different   2   1   0
- Described function of a microscope   1   0

Total Point Value: 25

> Step Eight: Consider resources, equipment, and materials that will be needed for effective instruction. Consider management strategies and safety issues.

Resources, Equipment, and Safety

- Make a list of books, videotapes, magazines, CDs, Web sites, and other resources that will provide background information for the concepts in the unit.
- Provide a list of resources—human resources, community resources, and experiences that will help teachers learn more about the topic.
- Make a list of equipment that will be needed for activities.
- List safety and management issues that need to be considered. Check to make sure safety precautions are clearly written into each of the activities in the unit.

EXAMPLE 2: APPLYING THE EIGHT STEPS TO A UNIT ON ROCKS AND MINERALS

Another approach to the development or modification of instructional materials for effective teaching in a K–12 program that might be of interest to a curriculum director or a development team is to begin with a holistic perspective of "what students should know and be able to do" related to a set of standards across grade levels. An outline for investigating Earth materials and forces within the Earth through a study of rocks and minerals is offered as a basis for discussion. The outline describes many features that might be included in K–12 units, but it may not include all of the features one would need to offer high quality instruction at a specific grade level.

Thought and Discussion

Activity: Considerations for Effective K–12 Instruction

1. Consider the ideas and suggestions for unit development presented for a unit on rocks and minerals and critique them using the indicators of high quality. Identify strengths and areas that need modification or improvement.

2. A range of activities that address standards at all grade levels is shown. Identify activities that would be useful for addressing the standards at your grade level. Identify activities, experiences, and resources that would need to be added.

   A sample activity for testing minerals to identify their unique properties is found at the end of this chapter. The model activity follows the Five E's format.

3. Suggest and record creative methods and strategies that would enhance a unit for your grade level. Share ideas and suggestions.

ROCKY ROADS—A STUDY OF ROCKS AND MINERALS

National Standards for K–4, 5–8, and 9–12

As a result of their activities in grades K–12 students should develop:

- Abilities necessary to do scientific inquiry
- Understanding about scientific inquiry

As a result of their activities in grades K–4, all students should develop an understanding of the properties of Earth materials.

- Earth materials are solid rocks and soils, water, and the gases of the atmosphere.
- Fossils provide evidence about the plants and animals that lived long ago and the nature of the environment at that time.

As a result of their activities in grades 5–8, all students should develop an understanding of the structure of the Earth system.

- Some changes in the solid Earth can be described as the "rock cycle." Old rocks at the Earth's surface weather form sediments that are buried, then are compacted, heated, and often recrystallized into new rock. Eventually, those new rocks may be brought to the surface by the forces that drive plate motions, and the rock cycle continues.

As a result of their activities in grades 9–12, all students should develop an understanding of geochemical cycles:

- Movement of matter between reservoirs is driven by the Earth's internal and external sources of energy. These movements are often accompanied by a change in the physical and chemical properties of matter.

Concepts from Benchmarks for Science Literacy (AAAS, 1993)

K–2: Chunks of rock come in many sizes and shapes, from boulders to grains of sand and even smaller. Change is something that happens to many things.

3–5: Rock is composed of different combinations of minerals.

6–8: Sedimentary rock buried deep enough may be reformed by pressure and heat, perhaps melting and recrystallizing into different kinds of rock. These reformed rock layers may be forced up again to become land surface and even mountains. Subsequently, this new rock too will erode. Rock bears evidence of the minerals, temperatures, and forces that created it.

9–12: The formation, weathering, sedimentation, and reformation of rock constitute a continuing "rock cycle" in which the total amount of material stays the same as its forms change.

Background Information

Vocabulary

The **crust** is the outermost layer of the Earth.

Elements are substances that contain only one kind of atom; they cannot be broken down into simpler substances.

Rocks are inorganic natural substances that form large parts of the Earth's crust. Some rocks are made almost entirely of one mineral, but in order for them to be classified as a mineral, they must be homogeneous. That is, they must have the same chemical composition throughout. Rocks contain more than one mineral.

A **mineral** is a homogeneous inorganic substance having a definite chemical composition. It is usually a solid but may be a liquid. Most minerals are formed by a combination of several elements, but some are homogeneous physically and chemically if they consist of elements of the same kind throughout. Minerals are identified on the basis of their physical and chemical properties. Common properties include color, luster, streak, crystal structure, hardness, cleavage, and density.

Igneous rocks are formed from melted rock that has cooled and solidified. Rocks buried deep in the Earth are acted upon by extreme heat and pressure and melt. The melted rock, called **magma,** may flow upward toward the Earth's crust and be ejected through a volcano. Magma that cools slowly forms large crystals; magma that cools rapidly forms very small crystals. Some common igneous rocks are granite, basalt, and obsidian.

Sedimentary rocks are formed in water or on land near the surface of the Earth. They are formed from the layering and eventual cementing of sediments. Sandstone, shale, limestone, and conglomerate are common sedimentary rocks.

Metamorphic rocks are formed when existing rocks are subjected to intense heat and pressure, which change them by transforming them into denser, more compact rocks. New minerals are created, and some metamorphic rocks appear banded or have a striped appearance. Some common metamorphic rocks are gneiss (from granite), marble (from limestone), and slate (from shale).

The **rock cycle** first offered by eminent geologist James Hutton (1727–1797) depicts the relationships that exist between igneous, sedimentary, and metamorphic rocks. The rock cycle shows the ways that rocks are recycled throughout the Earth's crust through a continuous process of change brought about by the processes of weathering, erosion, compaction, cementation, melting, and cooling.

Careers in Science

The science of studying rocks is called **petrology;** a scientist who studies rocks is a **petrologist.** Scientists who study minerals are **mineralogists.** They observe and define characteristics of minerals and explain their origins and development. Both types of scientists are geologists since geology studies the origin, composition, and evolution of the Earth. There are many careers related to rocks and minerals that students may research.

S-T-S Connections

Minerals and rocks play a vital role in the modern world. Based on current consumption rates, it is estimated that each person in the United States will use more than one million pounds of rocks, minerals, and metals in their lifetime! How, exactly, will you use them?

Some common minerals and their uses are:

- Lead—used in the making of batteries. Lead is used in radiation shielding during X-ray treatment by doctors and dentists, and it is also used as a protective shield on television screens. Lead is obtained from the ore galena (lead sulfide).
- Zinc—"copper" pennies are mostly zinc; zinc is used as an alloy metal with copper to make brass; it is used as a rust inhibitor for steel in the construction of cars, bridges, and ships.
- Copper—ores of copper are used to make brass, bronze, coins, jewelry, and cooking equipment; used for copper wire, which conducts electricity for home, appliances, cars, and so forth.
- Aluminum—the most abundant metal element in the Earth's crust; used to make cans, aircraft, sports equipment, electronic equipment, and appliances.
- Iron—used to make steel for cars, ships, cans, building materials, appliances, and so forth.
- Halite (salt)—used in food preservation, to enhance the taste of food, to melt ice on streets in winter, in manufacturing chemicals, for water treatment, and in papermaking; there are many other uses of salt.
- Limestone (calcium carbonate)—used as stone and in making cement; used in streets, roads, sidewalks, homes, and schools; used for decorative yard items; used in building construction.
- Coal—used in the generation of electricity; over 50 percent of all the electricity used in the United States is produced from coal-fired facilities.
- Flint—used by primitive people to make arrowheads, knives, and other types of tools necessary for survival; also used with steel as a fire starter.
- Gold—used in dentistry and medicine, art and jewelry, and medallions and coins; used in intricate circuitry for scientific and electronic instruments such as computers and in electroplating; the property of malleability allows gold to be thinner than a human hair.
- Silver—used in photography, jewelry, electronics, and currency; used in making mirrors, as plating for flatware and dishes, and in dental, medical, and scientific equipment.
- Feldspar—a rock-forming mineral; used in making glass, ceramics, enamelware, cement, roofing material, and soap.
- Quartz—found in all three types of rocks (igneous, sedimentary, and metamorphic); sand comes from quartz that has been weathered; some gems of quartz have been colored by other minerals, such as amethyst equals purple quartz and smoky quartz equals gray or black quartz; used for jewelry, lenses, and prisms.

- Talc—one of the softest minerals; used in the cosmetic industry and for making talcum powder; used as a filler in paper, insecticides, rubber, and paint.
- Graphite—dark in color with a metallic luster, graphite is another soft mineral; it is carbon, the same element as diamond, the hardest mineral; used as a natural lubricant and for lead in pencils.

A list of minerals and their properties may be found at the U.S. Geologic Survey Web site: http://pubs.usgs.gov/gip/gemstones/mneral.html

Some common rocks and their uses are:

- Obsidian—a black, glassy igneous rock, it is formed when lava cools suddenly; used to form knives, spearheads, and other sharp objects by early humans; used in jewelry and as a filler in garden soil.
- Pumice—white or gray, sponge-like igneous rock that forms when lava turns solid while gases are bubbling from it; it floats on water because of its porous texture; used as an abrasive.
- Marble—light-colored, coarse-grained metamorphic rock used for statues, monuments, building material, and tile for floors and walls.
- Slate—black or gray, fine-grained metamorphic rock; used for roofing and flagstone.
- Granite—light-colored, coarse-grained igneous rock formed inside the Earth; used in buildings, ornamental stone, monuments, and countertops.
- Sandstone—light, grainy sedimentary rock that is mostly quartz; used in construction, glass grinding, and sandblasting.

A description of rocks and suggestions for collecting them may be found at the U.S. Geologic Survey Web site: http://pubs.usgs.gov/gip/collect1/collect gip.html

A sample concept map that shows relationships between some of the important concepts for a unit on rocks and minerals is shown in Figure 9.6.

Context

Create a context for learning. Provide a variety of ways for students to get involved in a study of rocks and minerals. Some suggestions are described here.

- ***Establish relevance:*** To generate interest, give students an assignment to find examples of where rocks and minerals are found in and around their homes and their neighborhoods. Discuss the uses of rocks and minerals. Generate and record questions that students have about rocks and minerals. Identify misconceptions students have about them.
- ***Investigate as a scientist:*** Invite students to be part of a team of scientists studying rocks and minerals in an area of the country other than their own or in another country. (Optional: Research the research site and take a "virtual tour" of the area.) In preparation for the excursion, students may be provided with a few mineral samples to practice

Figure 9.6   Concept Map for Rocky Roads

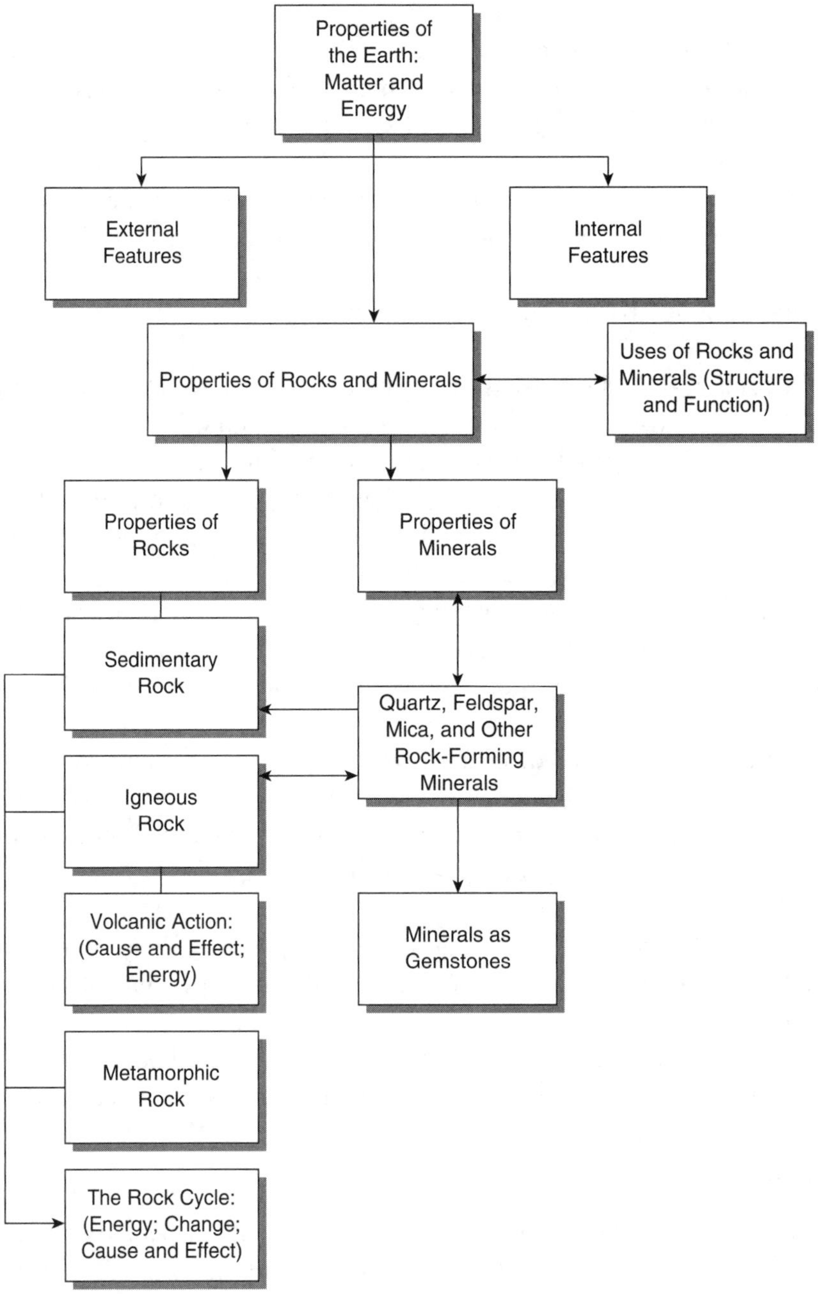

observing unique properties firsthand. A "field notebook" may be designed to record observations and drawings of the specimens.

- **_Visit a quarry:_** A field experience at a rock quarry will generate interest and questions and provide information about how rocks are removed from the Earth and used commercially. If possible, take students to a quarry where they can hunt for fossils in sedimentary rock.

- **_Visit an exhibit or museum:_** Exhibits and museum collections of rocks and minerals are fascinating to students of any age since they show unique and often amazing specimens of rocks, minerals, and gemstones.

Some museum pieces are very extraordinary and valuable. Take a virtual tour of museum specimens.

- *Investigate careers:* Research careers that are related to rocks and minerals. Allow students to develop action plans for studying rocks and minerals from the perspective of a career that interests them.

- *Connections to technology and society:* Begin the study of rocks and minerals from a commercial or environmental perspective, or both. Research the commercial uses of rocks and minerals. Discover how synthetic minerals, such as diamonds, are made and the commercial uses for such marvels of technology. What types of equipment are used to extract valuable minerals from the Earth? What are the trade-offs to mining minerals from under the ground? How cost-effective is the practice?

Identify inquiry questions related to goals and standards that arise through this approach and design activities to address them.

Learning Activities

Specific concepts need to be identified for the grade and ability levels of students, and each activity included in the unit needs to be carefully developed. Each activity should identify objectives and include relevant background information, inquiry questions, clear procedures, applications of learning, strategies for assessing learning, and suggestions for relearning and extended learning.

Sample Activities for Rocky Roads

Splish/Splash: How Much Land? How Much Water?

Students will investigate the relationship between the amount of land and water on Earth. They will complete a K-W-L about what makes up the crust of the Earth—ask questions; collect and interpret information.

E Is for Earth; E Is for Egg

An egg can be used as a model of the layers of solid material in the Earth. Through this activity, students can draw and label, create mental models, and visualize relationships. They learn that rocks are pieces of the materials that make up the Earth's crust.

Study of Favorite Rocks

An investigation of rocks can focus on their properties such as color, shape, size, mass, and so forth. Students can choose a "pet rock" to study or use locally found rocks to investigate, collect data, make generalizations, and show understanding.

Relationship Between Rocks and Minerals

This activity will provide an awareness that rocks are made up of minerals. Chocolate Chip Cookie Analogy—Analogical Thinking (create mental models)

Chocolate chip and nut cookies provide model "rocks" that can be dissected for their component "minerals." Students will observe, classify, and measure quantities; generalize; and comprehend/show understanding of the relationship between rocks and minerals.

Introduction to Fossils

Students should be introduced to fossils as part of a K–4 or 5–8 unit. They can observe and study a variety of plant and animal fossils. They can compare features of fossils with plants and animals of today.

Studying and Testing of Minerals

As students study an assortment of common minerals such as quartz, feldspar, mica, halite, graphite, coal, talc, copper, and others, they will identify basic properties. Students can conduct tests for color, streak, hardness, cleavage, specific gravity, and reaction to acid and make a detailed chart of their findings and use the chart to identify "unknowns." Students should research uses of minerals and recognize that they are nonrenewable resources. A lesson plan is provided for this activity later in this chapter.

Rocks and the Rock Cycle

Students will be introduced to the rock cycle as they study samples of igneous, sedimentary, and metamorphic rocks and identify their unique features. Students will investigate, collect data, generalize, compare/contrast, and apply their learning. Technology connections: Students will research commercial uses for rocks and minerals.

Volcanic Rocks

Students will study igneous rocks and identify their properties. They will identify igneous rock on the rock cycle diagram and trace the paths of change that occur over time. Mathematics connection: Students can study crystals and geometric solids.

Layered Rocks

Students will study sedimentary rocks, which are formed in water or on land near the surface of the Earth. A jar of material of various sizes (sand, gravel, silt) will be used to show how layers form. Sandstone and shale are common sedimentary rocks that show layering. Students should investigate fossils and ways that fossils are formed in sedimentary rock. Students will use the rock cycle diagram to trace the paths of change in sedimentary rock that occur over time.

Changed Rocks

Students will study metamorphic rocks and observe their unique properties. They will identify metamorphic rock on the rock cycle diagram and trace the paths of change that occur over time.

The Rock Cycle

Students will use rock samples to make a model of the rock cycle. They should investigate the sources of energy that drive the rock cycle and investigate the interrelationships between igneous, sedimentary, and metamorphic rocks and changes that occur throughout the cycle.

A more advanced study of the rock cycle will include the movement of matter between reservoirs in the Earth and identification of the internal and external sources of energy in the Earth that drive the movement. Students should identify the changes in physical and chemical properties of matter.

Notebooks to Record Information, Frame Thought, and Construct Meaning

All students should keep notebooks, which should be designed to "fit" the specific activities in the unit. Notebook entries will include background information, inquiry questions, procedures used in investigations and research, data and data tables, and explanations. An assortment of visuals, such as charts, pictures, diagrams, data tables, graphs, and graphic organizers, should be included to show evidence of thinking, doing, and learning.

Each investigation should be documented separately. Questions related to what was done, what was discovered, and what it means will be asked and answered for each activity. New questions, reflective thinking, and summaries of learning will also be included for each activity.

Differentiated Instructional Strategies

Instructional and management strategies may vary, based on student interest and needs as learners. Flexible grouping strategies include large or small group instruction and investigation and independent study. Students may need varied assignments, tiered activities, centers, contracts, or adjustments in the instructional plan to accommodate their learning styles, needs, and interests.

Tiered activities have the same objectives and focus but provide different approaches with varying degrees of difficulty to maximize the possibility that each student will learn concepts and skills and that each student will be appropriately challenged. Contracts allow students to choose alternative pathways and take responsibility for learning. Centers are useful for revisiting activities or for offering extended learning opportunities.

Multiple learning modalities should be used throughout instruction, including expository, hands-on activity, demonstrations, discussion, research, and open investigation. In addition, interest centers, reference books, trade books, videotapes, Web sites, and other resources need to be available for tiered and contractual learning.

Assessments for Learning

Formative assessments will provide evidence of learning. Continuous feedback should be given to students along with opportunities for relearning and extended learning. Notebook entiers are a source of evidence of learning. Other formative assessments may be embedded in the instructional activities and experiences.

Assessments of Learning

Assessment tasks show what students know and are able to do during or after instruction. Figure 9.7 provides some ideas for assessments.

Figure 9.7   Sample Assessments

Students will explain that the outermost portion of the Earth is composed of water and land and that the crust of the Earth (on top and under water) is made up of rock.	Students will use the rock cycle diagram to explain what might happen to any one of the components of the cycle over time.	Using the information in their notebooks, students will use a Venn diagram to show similarities and differences between a chocolate chip cookie and a rock.
Students will name and describe properties of three categories of rocks. They will give one example of a rock from each category and describe the properties that are common to the category.	At a higher level, students will describe the rock cycle in terms of the sources of energy that drive the cycle, cause/effect relationships throughout the cycle, and changes over time.	Students will show (actual object or drawing) one example of the rocks and/or minerals used in their home, school, community, or st

Activity: Identifying Rocks and Minerals

Overview

In this activity, students will conduct a series of tests on minerals to determine their properties. They will identify the color, luster, streak, hardness, and specific gravity for a set of minerals. Students will identify the minerals based on their properties.

Standards and Concepts

- Some changes in the solid Earth can be described as the rock cycle. Old rocks at the Earth's surface weather form sediments that are buried, then are compacted, heated, and often recrystallized into new rock. Eventually, those new rocks may be brought to the surface by the forces that drive plate motions, and the rock cycle continues.
- Fossils provide evidence about the plants and animals that lived long ago and the nature of the environment at that time.
- Movement of matter between reservoirs is driven by the Earth's internal and external sources of energy. These movements are often accompanied by a change in the physical and chemical properties of the matter.

Instructional Objectives

Following this activity, students will:

- Describe properties of minerals: color, luster, streak, hardness, and specific gravity
- Explain procedures for tests and describe the results of tests
- Use properties of minerals to identify them by name
- Identify some common uses for minerals

Materials and Safety

For each team of students: small samples of five of the minerals from Table 9.9 (sample kits may differ for each group of students or be the same); streak plate; copper penny, glass, and steel nail; balance and metric mass set; magnifiers; graduated cylinder; water

Inquiry Question

What are the properties of minerals? How is it possible to identify minerals by their properties? What are some ways that we use minerals in our daily lives?

Engagement

Create a context for studying minerals. Students might be invited to participate in a National Geographic Expedition to explore and mine minerals, or they may be asked to assist with setting up a display of minerals at a show. Establish a "need to know" about minerals based on the context.

Ask students what they know about minerals. Where have they seen minerals in their homes and neighborhoods?

Show students pictures or samples of minerals. Identify and discuss properties. Identify some similarities and differences in the samples.

Through discussion identify what students know and any misconceptions they have about minerals.

Review properties of matter, if necessary. Like all matter, minerals have specific properties that help to identify them. Some of the properties of minerals are color, luster, hardness, the color of the streak on a porcelain plate, and specific gravity.

Show examples of minerals with properties that students will be testing. Demonstrate the tests as needed. Challenge students to discover properties of the minerals in their sample kits and to identify the minerals by their properties.

Exploration

Testing Minerals: Conduct the following tests on one of the minerals in the sample kit. Record data in Table 9.7.

1. Color: Use a magnifier to observe the mineral's color; record the color in the data table.

2. Luster: Look at the sample in the light to determine if it has a metallic (metal-looking) or a nonmetallic (glassy, waxy, dull) luster. Record your observation.

3. Streak: Take an unglazed porcelain plate and drag the sample along the plate. The sample will leave a mark on the plate. The mark that is left by a streak is not always the same as the color of your sample. Record the color of the streak.

4. Hardness: The test for hardness can begin by using something as simple as your fingernail. If this does not scratch the sample, use something harder, like a copper penny and then a steel nail.

Use your fingernail (hardness: 2.5) to scratch the specimen. If it scratches the mineral, the hardness is about 2; if it does not, the hardness of the mineral is at least 2 to 2.5.

If a copper penny (3.5) scratches the specimen, its hardness is about 3.

If window glass (5.5) or a knife blade scratches the specimen, the hardness is less than 5.5.

If a steel file or nail (6.5) scratches the specimen, the hardness is less than 6.5.

If the streak plate (7) scratches the specimen, the hardness is a little less than 7.

Find the approximate hardness for each mineral specimen you are testing, and record the number on the data table.

Table 9.6 shows the Mohs Hardness Scale of minerals that have a hardness from 1 to 10, with 10 being the hardest mineral.

Table 9.6   Hardness Scale

Number	Mineral
10	Diamond
9	Corundum
8	Topaz
7	Quartz
6	Orthoclase
5	Apatite
4	Fluorite
3	Calcite
2	Gypsum
1	Talc

5. Specific Gravity: The next test requires you to find the specific gravity of the specimen and compare it to the specific gravity of water. The specific gravity of water is 1. Anything with a specific gravity less than 1 is less dense than water. Anything with a specific gravity more than 1 is denser than water.

Two measurements are needed to determine the specific gravity of a mineral: the mass in grams (g) and the volume in milliliters (mL). The specific gravity is found by dividing the mass of the specimen by the volume.

Use a balance and mass set to find the mass of the specimen. Mass = _____

Next drop the specimen into a graduated cylinder that contains 10 mL of water. Read the new volume.

Use the formula: New volume in mL − 10 mL = Volume of the mineral specimen

Once you know the mass and the volume of the sample, you can apply the formula:

specific gravity = mass divided by volume

Record the specific gravity.

Table 9.7   Data Table for Sample 1

Mineral Sample	Color	Luster	Streak	Hardness	Specific Gravity
Sample #1					

6. Repeat steps 1–5 for four additional mineral samples. Record data in Table 9.8.

Table 9.8   Data Table for Samples 2–5

Mineral Sample	Color	Luster	Streak	Hardness	Specific Gravity
Sample 2					
Sample 3					
Sample 4					
Sample 5					

Identifying Minerals

Now that you have discovered the properties of the mineral samples, you can use the information to identify them by name. Compare the characteristics of your minerals to those shown in Table 9.9. Can you identify them?

Uses of Minerals

Research the uses for the minerals you identified and others that are shown in Table 9.9. Identify at least three important uses for minerals.

Explanation

1. Describe the properties for each of the samples you tested. Were you able to identify the sample based on the properties you identified? Explain why or why not.

2. Describe the properties that were most unique to each of the minerals you identified.

3. Which minerals would you be able to identify again easily? Why?

4. Rocks contain a combination of minerals. Do you think it is possible to identify the minerals in rocks? Why or why not?

5. What are some uses for minerals?

Evaluation

1. Using your data table, describe the properties of one or more minerals.

2. Explain how you identified each of the properties.

3. Tell how you used properties to identify the minerals. Why were some minerals easier to identify than others?

4. Describe some common uses of minerals.

Table 9.9   Characteristics of Minerals

Mineral	Color	Luster	Streak	Hardness	Specific Gravity	Other
Biotite mica	Black	Glassy	Colorless	3	3.0	Fractures in thin plates
Pink feldspar	Pink	Glassy	White	6	2.7	Most common family
Quartz	Colorless; white	Glassy	None	7	2.7	Hexagonal crystal
Galena	Silver; black	Metallic	Gray	2.5	7.4	Ore of lead
Graphite	Silver	Metallic	Gray/black	1–2	2.2	Pencil "lead"
Halite	Colorless	Glassy		2.5	2.2	Rock salt; cubic
Hematite	Reddish brown	Dull/metallic	Resinous/ brown	5–6	5	Ore of iron
Pyrite	Brassy	Metallic	Gray/black	6.5	5.1	"Fool's gold"
Sulfur	Yellow	Resinous		2	2.1	Used in chemical industry; has distinct odor
Talc	White	Pearly	White	1	−2.7	Used in cosmetics

Elaboration and Extension

1. Research the crystalline structures of minerals, such as quartz, halite, and galena.

2. For what are synthetic minerals used? Learn more about the uses of minerals in industry.

3. Research natural gemstones. Where are gemstones found? How are they extracted from the Earth?

4. What characteristics of minerals make them good for jewelry? Find pictures of jewelry with gemstones. What makes gemstones like diamonds or emeralds expensive?

5. Investigate some careers related to minerals.

References

American Association for the Advancement of Science. (1993). *Project 2061: Benchmarks for science literacy.* New York: Oxford University Press.

Anderson, R. D. (2002). Reforming science teaching: What research says about inquiry, *Journal of Science Teacher Education, 13*(1), 1–12.

Armstrong, T. (1998). *Awakening genius in the classroom.* Alexandria, VA: Association for Supervision and Curriculum Development.

Armstrong, T. (2003). *The multiple intelligences of reading and writing.* Alexandria, VA: Association for Supervision and Curriculum Development.

Banks, J. A., Cookson, P., Gay, G., Hawley, W. D., Irvine, J. J., Nieto, S., (2001). Diversity within unity. *Phi Delta Kappan, 83*(3), 196–203.

Bellanca, J. (1995). *Designing professional development for change.* Arlington Heights, IL: IRI-SkyLight Training and Publishing.

Bellanca, J., & Fogarty, R. (2002). *Blueprints for achievement in the cooperative classroom.* Arlington Heights, IL: SkyLight Professional Development.

Birman, B. F., Desimone, L., Porter, A. D., & Garet, M. S. (2000). Designing professional development that works. *Educational Leadership, 58*(9), 28–32.

Black, P., & Wiliam, D. (1998). Inside the black box: Raising standards through classroom assessment. *Phi Delta Kappan, 79*(2), 139–148.

Blair, J. (2000). How teaching matters: Bringing the classroom back into discussion of teacher quality. *Education Week, 20*(8), 24.

Brophy, J. (1986). Teacher influences on student achievement. *American Psychologist, 41*(10), 1067–1077.

Burke, K. (2001). *Tips for managing your classroom.* Arlington Heights, IL: SkyLight Professional Development.

Bybee, R. W. (2002). *Learning science and the science of learning.* Alexandria, VA: National Science Teachers Association Press.

Caduto, M., & Bruchac, J. (1989). *Keepers of the earth: Native American stories and environmental activities for children.* Golden, CO: Fulcrum.

Caine, R. N., & Caine, G. (1991). *Teaching and the human brain.* Alexandria, VA: Association for Supervision and Curriculum Development.

Caine, R. N., & Caine, G. (1997). *Education on the edge of possibility.* Alexandria, VA: Association for Supervision and Curriculum Development.

Committee on Education. (2004). *Lost in space: Science education in New York City public schools.* Report from the Council of the City of New York.

Csikszentmihalyi, M. (1990). *Flow.* New York: Harper & Row.

Csikszentmihalyi, M. (1993). *The evolving self.* New York: HarperCollins.

Danielson, C. (2002). *Enhancing student achievement: A framework for school improvement.* Alexandria, VA: Association for Supervision and Curriculum Development.

Darling-Hammond, L. (1997). *The right to learn: A blueprint for creating schools that work.* San Francisco: Jossey-Bass.

Darling-Hammond, L., & McLaughlin, M. (1995). Policies that support professional development in an era of reform. *Phi Delta Kappan, 76*(8), 597–604.

DeHart Hurd, P. (1997). *Inventing science education for the new millennium.* New York: Teachers College Press.

Diamond, M., & Hopson, J. (1998). *Magic trees of the mind: How to nurture your child's intelligence, creativity, and healthy emotions from birth through adolescence.* New York: Penguin.

Enger, S., & Yager, R. E. (2001). *Assessing student understanding in science.* Thousand Oaks, CA: Corwin Press.

English, F. W. (1992). *Deciding what to teach and test.* Newbury Park, CA: Corwin Press.

Ermeling, B. A. (2005). *Transforming professional development for an American high school: A lesson study inspired, technology powered system for teacher learning.* Unpublished doctoral dissertation, University of California, Los Angeles.

Gabel, D. (1993). *Introductory science skills.* Prospect Heights, IL: Waveland Press.

Gardner, H. (1993). *Multiple intelligences: The theory in practice.* New York: Basic Books.

Gardner, H. (1999). *Intelligence reframed: Multiple intelligences for the 21st century.* New York: Basic Books.

Gartrell, J. E. (1989). *Methods of motion: An introduction to mechanics.* Alexandria, VA: National Science Teachers Association.

Gartrell, J. E., & Schafer, L. E. (1990). *Evidence of energy: An introduction to mechanics.* Alexandria, VA: National Science Teachers Association.

Gess-Newsome, J., & Lederman, N. (1999). *Examining pedagogical content knowledge.* Boston: Kluwer.

Goleman, D. (1995). *Emotional intelligence.* New York: Bantam Books.

Guskey, T. R. (2000). *Evaluating professional development.* Thousand Oaks, CA: Corwin Press.

Hammerman, E. (2005a). *Eight essentials of inquiry-based science.* Thousand Oaks, CA: Corwin Press.

Hammerman, E. (2005b). Linking classroom instruction and assessment to standardized testing. *Science Scope, 28*(4), 26–32.

Hammerman, E., & Musial, D. (1995). *Classroom 2061: Activity-based assessments in science.* Arlington Heights, IL: SkyLight Training and Publishing, Inc.

Harvard-Smithsonian Center for Astrophysics. (1995). *The private universe teacher workshop videos.* Burlington, VT: The Annenburg/CPB Math and Science Collection.

Hillen, J. (1991). Sea shells are special. *AIMS Newsletter, V*(8), 8-11.

Holloway, J. (2000). How does the brain learn science? *Educational Leadership, 58*(3), 85–86.

Inspiration Software, Inc. (2003, July). *Graphic organizers: A review of scientifically based research.* Portland, OR: Author. Prepared by the Institute for the Advancement of Research in Education. Retrieved February 13, 2006, from www.inspiration.com.

Jarrett, D. (1997, May). *Inquiry strategies for science and mathematics learning: It's just good teaching.* Portland, OR: Northwest Regional Education Laboratory.

Jeffers, S. (1991). *Brother eagle, sister sky: A message from Chief Seattle.* New York: Scholastic.

Jensen, E. (1989). *Teaching with the brain in mind.* Alexandria, VA: Association for Supervision and Curriculum Development.

Jensen, E. (2000). *Brain-based learning.* San Diego, CA: The Brain Store.

Joyce, B., & Showers, B. (1995). *Student achievement through staff development.* New York: Longman.

Klentschy, M., Garrison, L., & Amaral, O. M. (2001). *Valle imperial project in science (VIPS): Four-year comparison of student achievement data, 1995–1999.* El Centro, CA: El Centro School District.

Lantz, Jr., H. B. (2004). *Rubrics for assessing student achievement in science grades K–12.* Thousand Oaks, CA: Corwin Press.

Lapp, D. (2001). *Science link.* Washington, DC: National Science Resources Center.

Lieberman, A. (1995). Practices that support teacher development. *Phi Delta Kappan, 76*(8), 591–696.

Liem, T. (1987). *Invitations to science inquiry.* Lexington, MA: Ginn Press.

Loucks-Horsley, S. Hewson, P. W., Love, N., & Stiles, K. E. (1998). *Designing professional development for teachers of science and mathematics.* Thousand Oaks, CA: Corwin Press.

Macaulay, D. (1988). *The way things work.* Boston: Houghton Mifflin.

Macaulay, D. (2000). *Building big.* Boston: Houghton Mifflin.

Maddox, B. (2002). *Rosalind Franklin: The dark lady of DNA.* New York: HarperCollins Publishers.

Madrazo, G. (1998). Embracing diversity. *The Science Teacher, 65*(3), 20–23.

Marzano, R. J. (1991). Fostering thinking across the curriculum through knowledge restructuring. *Journal of Reading, 34*(7), 518–525.

Marzano, R. J., Pickering, D. J., & Pollock, J. E. (2001). *Classroom instruction that works.* Alexandria, VA: Association for Supervision and Curriculum Development.

McBer, H. (2000). *Research into teacher effectiveness: A model of teacher effectiveness* (Research Report #216). London: Department of Education and Employment.

McCormack, A. (1981). *Inventor's workshop.* Carthage, IL: Fearon Teacher Aids.

Musial, D., & Hammerman, E. (1992). Framing knowledge through moments: A model for teaching thinking in science. *Teaching thinking and problem solving, 14*(2), 12–15.

Musial, D., & Hammerman, E. (1997). *Framing ways of knowing in problem-based learning.* Unpublished manuscript.

National Commission on Mathematics and Science Teaching for the 21st Century. (2000). *Before it's too late.* Washington, DC: Author.

National Research Council. (1996). *National science education standards.* Washington, DC: National Academy Press.

National Research Council. (2000). *How people learn.* Washington, DC: National Academy Press.

National Science Resources Center. (1997). *Science for all.* Washington, DC: National Academy Press.

Parry, T., & Gregory, G. (1998). *Designing brain compatible learning.* Arlington Heights, IL: SkyLight Professional Development.

Peart, N. A., & Campbell, F. A. (1999). At-risk students' perception of teacher effectiveness. *Journal for a Just and Caring Education, 5*(3), 269–284.

Resnick, M. (2003). Playful learning and creative societies. *Education Update, 8*(6). Retrieved February 13, 2006, from www.educationupdate.com/archives/2003/feb03/issue/child_playfullrng.html

Ritchart, R. (2002). *Intellectual character: What it is, why it matters, and how to get it.* San Francisco: Jossey-Bass.

Rutherford, F. J., & Ahlgren, A. (1990). *Science for all Americans.* New York: Oxford University Press.

Shulman, L. S. (1986). Those who understand: Knowledge growth in teaching. *Educational Researcher, 15*(2), 4–14.

Sparks, D., & Hirsh, S. (1997). *A new vision for staff development.* Oxford, OH: National Staff Development Council.

Stronge, J. H. (2002). *Qualities of effective teachers.* Alexandria, VA: Association for Supervision and Curriculum Development.

Sylwester, R. (1995). *A celebration of neurons.* Alexandria, VA: Association for Supervision and Curriculum Development.

Sylwester, R. (2000). *A biological brain in a cultural classroom.* Thousand Oaks, CA: Corwin Press.

Tomlinson, C. (1999). *The differentiated classroom.* Alexandria, VA: Association for Supervision and Curriculum Development.

Tomlinson, C. A. (2004, March). *Balancing equity and excellence: Understanding the impact of educational decisions.* Paper presented at the 2004 NCREL Annual Conference, Naperville, IL.

Torp, L., & Sage, S. (1998). *Problems as possibilities.* Alexandria, VA: Association for Supervision and Curriculum Development.

Weiss, I. R., Pasley, J. D., Smith, S., Banilower, E. R., & Heck, D. J. (2003). *Looking inside the classroom: A study of K-12 mathematics and science education in the United States.* Chapel Hill, NC: Horizon Research.

Wenglinsky, H. (2000, October). *How teaching matters: Bringing the classroom back into discussions of teacher quality.* Princeton, NJ: Educational Testing Service, Policy Information Center.

Wolfe, P. (2001). *Brain matters.* Alexandria, VA: Association for Supervision and Curriculum Development.

Index

**CORWIN
PRESS**

The Corwin Press logo—a raven striding across an open book—represents the union of courage and learning. Corwin Press is committed to improving education for all learners by publishing books and other professional development resources for those serving the field of PreK–12 education. By providing practical, hands-on materials, Corwin Press continues to carry out the promise of its motto: **"Helping Educators Do Their Work Better."**